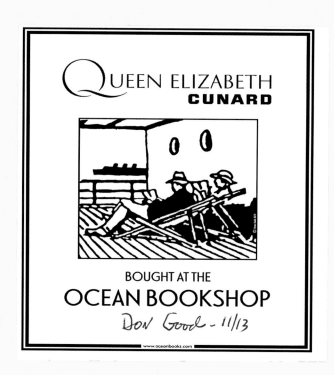

QUEEN ELIZABETH
CUNARD

BOUGHT AT THE
OCEAN BOOKSHOP

Don Good - 11/13

www.oceanbooks.com

CUNARD

QUEEN ELIZABETH

A CELEBRATION OF OCEAN TRAVEL
FOR MODERN ELIZABETHAN TIMES

PHILIP DAWSON

Published by: Ferry Publications, PO Box 33, Ramsey, Isle of Man IM99 4LP

Tel: +44 (0) 1624 898445   Fax: +44 (0) 1624 898449   E-mail: ferrypubs@manx.net   Website: www.ferrypubs.co.uk

Published by:

Ferry Publications, PO Box 33, Ramsey, Isle of Man IM99 4LP

Tel: +44 (0) 1624 898446   Fax: +44 (0) 1624 898449

E-mail: ferrypubs@manx.net   Website: www.ferrypubs.co.uk

CONTENTS

Produced and designed by Ferry Publications trading as Lily Publications Ltd

PO Box 33, Ramsey, Isle of Man, British Isles, IM99 4LP

Tel: +44 (0) 1624 898446   Fax: +44 (0) 1624 898449

www.ferrypubs.co.uk   E-Mail: info@lilypublications.co.uk

Printed and bound by Gomer Press Ltd., Wales, UK +44 (0) 1559 362371 © Lily Publications 2010

First Published: October 2010

Second Edition: December 2010

Third Edition: December 2011

*The **Queen Elizabeth** at a late stage of fitting out, with most major structural work already completed and the funnel and mast in place. (Brian David Smith)*

INTRODUCTION

BY PHILIP DAWSON

It is a pleasure, indeed a privilege, to present this second work on the new Cunard Queens, following our first title in the series, '*Cunard Queen Victoria: A celebration of tradition for twenty-first century ocean travel*' published earlier this year. The subject of this volume, the new *Queen Elizabeth*, is likewise a very special ship, perhaps even the more so for the influence of Queen Victoria's success, for her significant historical links with the first *Queen Elizabeth* built some 70 years earlier, and for the Royal Family's long association with the Cunard Line and its ships. With the one exception of the *Queen Victoria*, named by the Duchess of Cornwall at Southampton in late 2007, five Cunard Queens have been launched or named by the Queens on the throne at the time of their building, with the *QE2*, the *Queen Mary 2* and the new *Queen Elizabeth* all being so honoured by the present reigning Monarch during the new Elizabethan era of her illustrious reign.

Although structurally and technologically belonging to Cunard's corporate parent's Carnival's luxury Vista series, delivered in tailored renditions to Holland America, P&O, Costa and Cunard, the new *Queens Victoria* and 'Elizabeth' are distinctively unique as Cunard ships and as fleet mates to the Line's flagship *Queen Mary 2* built specifically for the dual role of seasonal express North Atlantic service as well as worldwide cruising. While being sister ships of the same building class, the *Queen Victoria* and *Queen Elizabeth*, built three years apart, differ in much the same way that the first Mary and Elizabeth had their own very distinctive

characters, partly attributable to the four-year span between their completions, though the first Elizabeth only embarked her first paying passengers after seven years of wartime national service.

Apart from their initial four wooden-hulled paddle steamers needed to start up the original transatlantic postal service commissioned by the Admiralty in 1840, Cunard has tended to build its principal passenger fleet individually and service proven before sisters of the same type were laid down. The sister ships *Persia* and *Scotia*, that introduced a superlative standard of comfort at their time, and

*With her bow set towards the open Adriatic Sea on the afternoon of 30th September 2010, Cunard's new **Queen Elizabeth** takes her leave of Fincantieri's Monfalcone Shipyard where she was built. (Brian David Smith)*

coincidentally Cunard's last paddle steamers, were built six years apart in 1856 and 1862 respectively. Though ordered as a pair 'Pretty Sisters' *Caronia* and *Carmania* of 1905 differed in that the *Carmania* was powered by steam turbines to test the then newfangled machinery's effectiveness before committing to its use two years later aboard the larger record-breaking *Lusitania* and *Mauretania*. Built simultaneously by John Brown & Company Ltd (Clydebank) and Swan Hunter & Wigham Richardson (Wallsend-on-Tyne), these too differed in many details of their plan and building as well as by the architecture of their interiors and ultimately in their characters. The 11-year time span between the debuts of the first *Queens Mary* and 'Elizabeth' also bridged the generational gap between the pre- and post-war eras and the significant changes in society, especially on the Atlantic's British and European side.

In many ways the new *Queen Elizabeth* shows the same sort of refinement in detail over the *Queen Victoria* that distinguished the first Elizabeth from the *Queen Mary*. Now as then, these are differences that set two sister ships apart, one from the other, more by their character and personality yet without doing so to the detriment of one or the other. Remarkably, the new Elizabeth shows a similarly gentle lightening of the overall interior palette over that of the Victoria as her namesake of 70 years earlier had revealed in comparison with the *Queen Mary*. The service relationship between the new 'Victoria' and 'Elizabeth' shows promise of being similar to that between the original Queens, where both being universally popular though with repeat passengers developing their own special allegiances with one or the other.

Our story begins with round-trip Atlantic crossings in 1948 on the first 'Elizabeth' where we introduce a number of characters that are composites of people known to the author and whose lives we briefly follow through the time span between this voyage and the new Elizabeth's debut in late 2010. Having provided a detailed description of the *Queen Victoria* in the first book of this series, we concentrate here rather on the differences in, and special features of, the new ship and present a more detailed account of her building and entry into service. For this reason we take the perhaps unusual approach of discussing the *Queen Elizabeth*'s amenities, interiors and decoration before chronicling her construction. We conclude with her naming by HM The Queen at Southampton and look at the Royal Family's long association with the Cunard Line and with the Nation's ships and shipping in general before wishing the *Queen Elizabeth* 'bon voyage' as she commences her maiden voyage to the Atlantic Islands.

As the *Queen Elizabeth*'s paint is still fresh and there is that characteristic elan of pristine newness throughout the ship we are delighted to offer this brief journey through the creation and inauguration of the third new Cunard Queen to be brought into service in the incredibly short time span of only seven years. We hope that you will enjoy this story of the ship's creation as much as we have enjoyed presenting it.

Philip Dawson,
Toronto, October 2010

*The first **Queen Elizabeth** in a romantic painting showing her against a backdrop of the Lower Manhattan skyscrapers with the Woolworth Building appearing above the ship's bridge. (Courtesy of Cunard)*

CHAPTER 1

SETTING THE SCENE

CUNARD

QUEEN ELIZABE

Shortly after 06.00 on the morning of Thursday 22nd April 1948, the Cunard White Star Line's *Queen Elizabeth*, quietly slipped her mooring lines and departed from Southampton at the beginning of a regular peacetime voyage to New York, fully booked with 2,283 passengers on board. Having made her maiden commercial voyage in October 1946, after six relentless years of troop-carrying service during World War II, she was then the world's largest ship and the newest liner on the premiere express transatlantic run between Europe and North America. Her slightly older sister, the *Queen Mary* had also been extensively refurbished following her wartime service and reinstated to peacetime commercial service in July 1947, at long last realising Cunard's ultimate ambition of a two-ship express transatlantic service with regular weekly sailings in both directions.

The emergence of Cunard's great *Queens* on their regular North Atlantic trade signalled a welcome return to normality and a sense of *business as usual* after the tumultuous upheaval, destruction and misery brought by six years of war that had implicated the ordinary civilian populations of Britain and Europe as no event in history had ever done. As the battleship grey and khaki of wartime service finally gave way to Cunard's familiar black hull, white superstructure and red-and-black funnels, there was a renewed sense of being re-connected with the outside world and the hope that things might again be as they once were, at least for the time being.

The *Queen Mary*'s pre-war French Line counterpart, the *Normandie* was gutted by fire at her New York pier in 1942, where after a monumental salvage effort lasting until autumn the following year, her hull was finally righted, re-floated and towed away, first to Brooklyn's Navy Yard and then to Port Newark where she was finally broken up in 1947. The veteran *Ile de France* was restored to commercial

Top: The first **Queen Elizabeth**'s *hull atop the inclined launch ways at Clydebank shortly before the ship's launch in September 1938. (Bruce Peter collection)*

Above: The first **Queen Elizabeth** *in battleship grey as the ship appeared during the first six years of her life in wartime service as a troop carrier. (Bruce Peter collection)*

service in July 1949 and joined a year later by North German Lloyd's former *Europa*, awarded to France in reparation for *Normandie*'s loss, and extensively modernised and refitted in France as the *Liberté*. The United States Lines and Holland America flagships *America* and *Nieuw Amsterdam* returned to their regular North Atlantic trades in 1946 and 1947 respectively.

Meanwhile, Cunard had the biggest post-war fleet and the largest ships on the Atlantic, with the greatest variety of sailings and schedules as well as some of the finest accommodation and service available at sea anywhere. Thanks to their outstanding wartime service the *Queens* were already veritable legends in their own times, with the established long-term service record of the Line also to their credit. During 1948 Cunard carried 197,772 passengers, of which about 150,000 travelled aboard the *Queens*.[1] By the

*The first **Queen Elizabeth** and the **Queen Mary** in peace- and wartime colours in 1946 as the **Queen Elizabeth** (left) prepares for commercial service and the **Queen Mary** (right) returns home for restoration to her former glory. (John Hendy collection)*

mid 1950s the Line was carrying about a third of all transatlantic passengers. The *Queen Elizabeth* was then the world's largest ship, and until the *United States* completed her maiden east- and westbound maiden voyages in 1952, the only slightly smaller *Queen Mary* was the fastest liner afloat.

As the *Queen Elizabeth* made her 22nd April 1948 departure from Southampton, passengers in all three passenger classes found themselves to be in a veritable wonderland of luxury, comfort and plenty, contrasting greatly with the immediate post-war drabness of Britain and Europe. Even the modest price of a single tourist class ticket for a berth in a shared cabin bought four-and-a-half days of blissful respite from the trials and tribulations of the outside world. No vestigial remnant of war remained aboard either of the meticulously refurbished and freshly repainted *Queens* save perhaps a halo effect of their illustrious wartime services, credited by Britain's wartime Prime Minister Sir Winston Churchill with shortening the war by a year[2] thanks to their huge carrying capacities and great speed. Most of the *Queen Elizabeth*'s interior fittings and furnishings were in fact virtually brand new, having been left behind when the ship made her secretive dash to New York in 1940 or were removed during the conversion for trooping in New York and stored throughout the war years.

The *Queen Elizabeth*'s passengers had embarked the previous evening, most of them having travelled on one of four special *boat trains* leaving from London's Waterloo Station between 16.49 and 19.00 and taking them directly to the Southampton Western Docks. The new Ocean Terminal, designed specifically for the *Queens* and other large liners, was to open in 1950. Dinner on board that evening while still alongside Pier 101 would offer a welcoming first experience of the bounteous cuisine that would be a high point of the voyage. Rationing- and shortages-weary Britons in particular were amazed at the seemingly inexhaustible quantities of even such ordinary things as white bread and butter, let alone the beef steaks, veal, fresh salmon, poultry and the more exotic items like oysters and caviar served in First Class. Fresh Florida grapefruits and oranges, along with various seasonal fruits were a sheer delight and there was a whole generation of children aboard for whom ice cream and sweets were something altogether new. In the early post-war years ships' doctors were kept busy dealing with digestive problems experienced by passengers long unaccustomed to such copious quantities of rich food. The breakfast menu, for instance, offered ten choices of cereal and three types of bacon. Remarkably, dinner rolls were a particularly popular item as the white flour used for baking them was in short supply. These were an especially welcome gift often given to those visiting ocean-going ships in British ports. When King George VI and Queen Elizabeth paid a visit to the *Queen Elizabeth* at Southampton in July 1948, one of three gift parcels of goodies from the ship sent ashore with the Royal party was labelled 'Rolls'.[3] Like most ships at the time, the Cunard *Queens* were victualled and provisioned for the round-trip in New York, where wartime shortages had been a far less serious issue in the United States.

Once the *Queen Elizabeth* was underway that morning, there would be a rush on the ship's shops, particularly to buy items of clothing, rationed in the UK until March 1949. Business men going abroad from Britain, in particular, were keen to convey the right impression of a prosperous new era, suited out in British-made clothing manufactured for export and unavailable at home. Ladies were keen to pursue the *New Look* of Christian Dior's Corolle Line collection introduced in 1947, or if nothing else, eager at least to buy stockings, and at long last the then new *nylons!*

As normal peacetime industry and commerce resumed,

*The first **Queen Elizabeth** making a turnaround at the Southampton Ocean Terminal in the sixties with her Number 2 forward hatch open, and various working gangways to D deck for provisioning and stores handling. (FotoFlite)*

*Top: The first **Queen Elizabeth**'s first-class lounge was typical of the visual warmth of the ship's richly veneered interiors, indirect lighting schemes and plush furnishings that conveyed a sense of comfortably elegant British post-war modernity. (Bruce Peter collection)*

*Above: The first **Queen Elizabeth** showing a hotel-style first class double cabin with a lady passenger at the dressing table, preparing perhaps for the evening's Captain's reception or formal dinner and ball. (Bruce Peter collection)*

there were large numbers of business people travelling in First and Cabin Class, back and forth across the Atlantic in the course of their work. The big liners then provided the only equivalent of today's business air travel, at a time when even basic transatlantic telephone service was expensive and in many instances calls had to be booked ahead of time, and long before the advent of other technological conveniences of today such as teleconferencing, mobile phones, email and the Internet. For these people the *Queens* provided the advantage of, in effect, being able to cross from continent to continent over what amounted to little more than a long weekend at sea. Back then, when the pace of doing business was less hard-driven, the crossing could be enjoyed as a respite to prepare one's mind for the business ahead or to unwind on the voyage home after its completion. Nobody had heard of jetlag then as the ship's clocks were put forward or back one hour each night during the voyage.

Numerous British ex-servicemen who had married and were starting families found that their most promising option was to seek their fortunes abroad in countries such as Australia, Canada and the United States. These were people emigrating on their own apart from those voyages provided aboard the *Queen Mary* for brides and children of American servicemen. Derek, a draftsman from the Midlands, who had ended up as an army lieutenant with the occupying forces in Berlin at the War's end had met Allison there, where she was stationed as a nurse, and married her later in 1945 while they were both on leave in England.

After being doubled up with Allison's parents at their war-damaged home in London-Blackheath, they and their two-year-old daughter Gillian and ten-month-old son Richard were booked in a four-berth tourist class inside cabin on C Deck, bound for New York and the hopes of a brighter future in America. They would go to Chicago,

Illinois where Derek had an uncle in the general contracting business who had offered to help the young family get started. They were thrilled with the service and home comforts of the *Queen Elizabeth*, and with the pleasures of the table, which all but brought Allison to tears of joy that first morning as the great liner steamed past the Isle of Wight for dreamlike offerings of fruit and real freshly squeezed orange juice. Gill, who celebrated her second birthday on board, made herself sick on ice cream, soda pop and chocolate cake.

The outbound call at Cherbourg was made at midday, with passengers and mail from the Continent then still having to be embarked by tender – it would be another four years before reconstruction and dredging of the war-damaged French port would be completed and the Cunard *Queens* could be docked starting in May 1952.[4] Among the European passengers who boarded the *Queen Elizabeth* that first afternoon of the voyage there were many more taking leave of a troubled and severely devastated Continent, likewise seeking the chance of personal peace and prosperity in the New World. These included a number of families from the Netherlands responding to the call of their national government for those willing, and able to do so, to emigrate at least for the time while the Netherlands rebuilt and revitalised after the heavy wartime destruction of their homeland. The nation's resources were also besieged by an influx of those displaced by Japanese occupation of its possessions in the East Indies. Later the Dutch government would handle much of this trade with its own ships operated under Holland America Line's direction.

As the *Queen Elizabeth* sped westwards across the North Atlantic for the next four days, those aboard, regardless of which class they had booked, could relax in a secure atmosphere of comfort and prosperity. A subdued sense of

Allied victory lingered as the world once again settled back into peacetime living, and for those emigrating from the United Kingdom, the ship's very British style of service was a fond and long to be remembered parting gesture of a beloved homeland and cherished way of life. On Tuesday morning, 27th April, Derek, Allison and the children set foot on American soil for the first time as they stepped from the gangway onto Pier 90 in New York City. All passengers were landed directly at Pier 90 after completing passport inspections and immigration formalities on board the ship. After the National Origins Act of 1924 came into effect, only displaced persons and war refugees still had to be processed through Ellis Island until it closed in 1954.

As they and the children stepped from the gangway, Derek was wearing the new woollen cardigan and white linen shirt he had bought on board, and Allison was in her first-ever pair of nylons and the new outfit from Selfridges purchased in London with the last of her clothing coupons for the family's grand arrival in America. Once through US Customs and with arrangements made at the pier for their trunks to be forwarded by Rail Express, the family took a taxi to Grand Central Station for the long wait until the *20th Century Limited* overnight train's 18.00 departure that evening for Chicago. As it turned out one of the Dutch families, Henrik, Tina and their three children, would be aboard the same train on their way to Minneapolis. Dolfus and Lisa from somewhere near Eindhoven, who had been seated at the same dining table as Derek and Allison during the voyage, would be heading across the Canadian border from Penn Station to Toronto to join fellow countrymen from the Netherlands already settled as farmers in the nearby town of Bowmanville. Before dispersing from the ship to their various destinations, everyone had already exchanged addresses of the friends and relatives at their destinations with promises to write letters and send

13

*The first **Queen Elizabeth** underway in the English Channel, probably at the outset of a crossing to New York early in her career before the swimming pool and lido were added and some of her lifeboats replaced with excursion launches for cruising. (FotoFlite)*

Christmas cards. That evening as they ate their supper in the bright and cheerful surroundings of the train's streamlined modern dining car, Allison and Derek already felt reassured that they had made a good choice in bringing their young family to this hospitable and prosperous land where they would make their new home and lives.

The *Queen Elizabeth* would remain tied up at Pier 90 for little more than 48 hours, before setting her bows eastwards on the midday tide for her return voyage to Southampton, with a brief call to land passengers and mail at Cherbourg. Again the ship was full, with some two thousand passengers and their baggage, along with mails and a small amount of specialised cargo all being loaded during the morning hours before sailing. Again First and Cabin Classes would be mainly populated with the usual mix of celebrities and business people going about their regular affairs. With the high season approaching, tourist cabins were already filling up with those wanting to visit family and friends 'across the pond' or take holidays in Europe. Ex-service personnel were keen to return to places where they had served and other *war buffs* were anxious to visit the sites where history had been made – there would still be plenty for them to see, as much of Europe was the colossal site of a still badly scarred battlefield. Later that summer, the 1948 Olympic Games would bring athletes, officials and thousands of spectators to London during the first two weeks of August.

There were also those aboard returning home from periods of self-imposed exile in North America to rekindle lives and livelihoods in their victorious or liberated homelands. Meagan and Roger were returning to their home in Cornwall after Roger had accepted a four-year contract with an engineering firm in Colorado and arrived on one of the *Queen Mary*'s last voyages before war was declared in 1939. Unable to return to England in 1943, Roger renewed his contract for a further four years. It had then taken an additional six months to get passage back to England. As much as they had enjoyed their time in Colorado, Meagan in particular yearned for the English countryside she so loved and to be back in her own home. Her mother had looked after the house during the war and had taken in a retired couple evacuated from London during the Blitz who stayed and helped her look after the place until the War's end.

Ushi (short for Ursula), a single woman in her mid thirties, who had fled Germany during the late 1930s, was on her way home aboard the *Queen Elizabeth* to salvage her family's property and hotel near the north German seaside resort centre of Kiel. Fearful that war was imminent, she had sailed to New York from Le Havre in 1938 aboard the *Ile de France* and had spent ten years helping her older brother run a lakeside resort in Upstate Wisconsin. With the benefit of that experience she was anxious to return home with new ideas in North American style hospitality that she felt would attract foreign visitors to the family establishment in years to come.

After finishing their dinner at the early sitting one evening during the crossing, Meagan and Roger stepped from the warm glow of the Promenade Deck main foyer's lights into the natural half-light of the port-side Promenade Deck to admire the evening sky in the red afterglow of a sunny day through its large windows. Holding hands on the rail beneath the glass pane they mused at the scene's symbolism of a chapter in their lives coming to a close and another about to open. Meagan recalled the joy of watching the twilight during long summer evenings from the home to which they were returning. A few panes further away Ushi stood alone with her own thoughts in a similar vein, and recollections of summer evenings on the Baltic coast when her family's hotel would be filled with guests dancing on the terrace overlooking Kiel Bay on evenings such as this. Meagan spotted her and asked her to join them for an after-dinner drink up forward in the Observation Lounge overlooking the ship's bows. Later in the ladies room Ushi told Meagan that she was trying to make the most of the voyage before returning home where she would probably have to settle for a steady diet of steamed fish, sausage and sauerkraut, and get around riding a bicycle if she would be lucky enough even to get one. The three became friends, with Meagan and Roger inviting Ushi to come to their home when she needed a holiday, and she in turn insisted that they would stay free for as long as they liked as her first guests when she reopened the hotel.

On the deck below a group of American ex-servicemen with their young wives were drinking beer and soda pop in

15

*The first **Queen Elizabeth** makes her approach to the landing stage at Cherbourg with gangway doors in the ship's side to the upper foyer on A Deck already opened in readiness for the transfer of passengers in France. (John Hendy collection)*

the Tourist Class Winter Garden, on their way back to Europe for a holiday. For the girls it would firstly be a welcome return home to see their families in Britain, while the men were looking forward to seeing more of London and Paris with the time to enjoy their sights and a bit of the night life. There would of course be a seaside trip to Normandy to relive the glories of the D-Day landings, show their wives where they had done their heroic deeds towards the liberation of Europe and perhaps see if there was still shrapnel to be found on the beaches.

As the *Queen Elizabeth* approached Cherbourg on

Tuesday 4th May, Ushi had her hair and a manicure done in the beauty salon and stocked up on toiletries, cosmetics and nylons in the ship's shops. She would land by tender at Cherbourg early that evening, where she would spend the night at a pension before starting her rail journey home to Kiel, changing trains in Paris, Brussels, Osnabrück and Hamburg. The ship would arrive in Southampton around midnight, being slightly less dependent on making the high tide with partially depleted fuel tanks and stores, marginally reducing her draft. Passengers would disembark on Wednesday morning, where Meagan and Roger would be met by relatives who would drive them home. The party of American ex-GIs and their wives had bought tickets on board for the special train from the pier to London's Waterloo Station.

The Cunard Line and particularly the *Queens* at that time were far more than merely a shipping line and the world's two largest liners – they were a veritable institution. The *Queens* were always especially loved by American passengers, for whom they conveyed the quintessence of things British. In a story carried by the 'London Observer' in the latter years of the *Queen Elizabeth*'s career, the English author Eric Newby pointed out that: 'Not only to the British but to multitudes of Americans who travel in her for a foretaste of what they believe to be the British way of life, (the ship) is perhaps the only part of their visit that lives up to the expectation.'[5]

Towards a new era

Cunard's own new Elizabethan era, during which there have now been three *Elizabeths*, including the *QE2* and now the new *Queen Elizabeth*, in effect began when their first *Queen Elizabeth* made her October 1946 maiden voyage to New York in the regular revenue-earning passenger service for which she was designed and built. By that time the Line had already been in business for just over a hundred years, commencing at the outset of the likewise illustrious Victorian age that generally coincided with the broader world phenomenon of the Second Industrial Revolution.

It was Cunard that had first set the pattern for regular scheduled steamship service across the Atlantic Ocean in 1840, three years after Queen Victoria's coronation, with the assurance of 'speed, comfort and safety'[6] sustaining swift and regular passage of the Royal Mail and its passengers by steamship from one side of the North Atlantic Ocean to the other. It was always these values, with an especially strong

emphasis on safety, which motivated all development of the Line and its fleet. While keeping pace with the commercial competition that it inevitably attracted, the design and building of Cunard ships was motivated primarily by the need to carry given quantities of mail and numbers of passengers in the smallest and most economical ships that would meet the requirements of speed, comfort and safety.

Yet, from its bold beginnings as a pioneer in steam shipping, the Line always remained commercially progressive in the design of its ships. Through the Victorian years of 1837 to 1901 steam shipping progressed from pioneering wooden-hulled paddle steamers such as Cunard's modest *Britannia* and her three sisters that inaugurated the Line's mail and passenger service between Liverpool, Halifax and Boston to screw propulsion, iron, then steel hulls, and ever greater speeds and carrying capacities. The steam turbine's invention by Charles Algernon Parsons was Victoriana's lasting final contribution to the march of shipbuilding progress that set the pace for onward development well into the coming twentieth century.

Known as 'the pretty sisters', the functionally attractive *Caronia* and *Carmania* of 1905 were among the first to be built with more dominant modern superstructures. Newfangled Parsons steam turbines were cautiously first tried aboard the *Carmania* before committing to their use for the record-breaking express liners *Lusitania* and *Mauretania*, that decisively wrested the Blue Riband honours for speed back from Hamburg America Line's *Deutschland* in 1907. Yet as Cunard, and for that matter most of their competitors, absorbed twentieth-century technological advancement in naval architecture and marine engineering, shipboard living remained firmly rooted in the institutions of Victorian hotelier *grand luxe* through what amounted to a lingering half life of that era's highly stratified social structures ashore that lasted until the 1939 outbreak of World War II.

Apart from the masses emigrating to the New World and then still comparatively small number of those travelling in the line of their work as cabin- or second-class passengers in what amounted to the *business class* of its time, discretionary luxury travel remained for the most part a privilege of the wealthy – these were the people who stayed at the London or Paris Ritz, The Adlon or Kempinski in Berlin or New York's Waldorf Astoria, and who booked luxury suites aboard the fastest and most prestigious liners when they *crossed* between the Old and New Worlds. They were the *frequent travellers* of an age when it was also important that they were seen to be travelling well and observing all of the correct etiquette for every occasion of their movements. One was expected to be good at the social art of conversation with an adequate knowledge of the classics. Full formal attire was mandatory for Captain's dinners, with decorations, for gentlemen, socially disadvantaging those lacking a military background, the medals and ribbons to show for it[7] – all of this also served to thwart wannabe interlopers from the lower classes eager to try mingling with the on-board rich and famous.

So far as the ships themselves were concerned, the layout of the *Caronia* and *Carmania* set the standard for Cunard, and for that matter much of their competition, right through the next 40 years or so to the *grand luxe* era's post World War II sunset. The first class public rooms usually featured a large main lounge amidships with the smoking room aft and a smaller library- or parlour-lounge forward, and flanked by the Promenade Deck to either side and with an open-air Verandah Café aft. In addition to the stratification of shipboard living by class, there remained also separate spheres of male and female social activity, with the forward salon accepted as being the ladies lounge and the smoking room generally more overtly restricted to 'Gentlemen only, please'.

Expanded and enhanced renditions of these layouts were adopted for the pre World War I *Lusitania*, *Mauretania* and the larger *Aquitania*, and ultimately in the 1930s for the first *Queens*, *Mary* and *Elizabeth*, along with the smaller second *Mauretania* of 1939 and *Caronia* only completed in 1949. Within the considerably larger scale of the *Queens*, forward-facing Observation Lounges, with cocktail bars and an outlook over the ship's bows through the forward end of the enclosed Promenade Deck were added. The exclusive Grill Room introduced as a surcharged dining option aboard the *Aquitania* for first class passengers was significantly upgraded and enhanced as the Verandah Grill with both full-service dining facilities and provision for light entertainment and dancing aboard both the *Mary* and the *Elizabeth*. These added significantly to the diversity of life on board with greater opportunity for social contact among passengers of both sexes.

Cunard tended to leave *moderne* and the avant-guard to its European competitors and continued to maintain a strong sense of its well-established and commercially successful traditional image through the 1930s, while French Line's *Normandie* and the Holland America *Nieuw Amsterdam* were taking a somewhat more informal approach to luxury first-class North Atlantic travel. By the time the *Queen Mary* made her May 1936 debut, the *Normandie* had already introduced the era of the 80,000-ton Atlantic superliner and had a year's service experience to her credit to show for it. Having no wish to compete with the new French Line flagship's structural daring with its vast open-plan interior spaces and axial layout following the hull's centreline, Cunard's design people nonetheless were keen to observe their competition's ships and the general march of engineering and technological progress with a view to achieving detailed planning of their second *Queen*-class liner.

The *Queen Elizabeth* was designed with 12 high-performance superheated boilers in place of the *Mary*'s 24,[8] and thus needed only two, rather than three, funnels. This in turn created greater expanses of uninterrupted space inside the ship, providing for a more straightforward plan of the main Promenade Deck public spaces. There was a greater emphasis on large rectangular rooms and less space having to be given over to the galleries needed as circulating spaces bypassing the funnel uptakes. The added space gained from the two-funnel plan and more cohesive interior layout provided for a cinema to be added with no loss of capacity for other public rooms. The *Queen Elizabeth*'s architectural design and interior decoration generally followed as a more minimalist rendition of the streamlined modernistic thirties styling of the *Mary*, according the newer ship a more refined leitmotif. As the travelling public only got its first look at this ship after the War, her comparative modernity was mistakenly attributed by many as merely being post-war austerity. Where the *Queen Mary*'s lead architect Benjamin Morris was an American who brought an element of jazzy New York panache to the *Mary*, London architect George Grey Wornum asserted a more understated British *creative signature* aboard the *Elizabeth*, reflecting his then recent design of the Royal Incorporation of British Architects (RIBA) building at London's Portland Place.

Following the *Normandie*'s example, a change was also made from the traditional arrangement of ventilator housings along the *Queen Mary*'s top decks to a concentration of all air intakes and outlets into fan housings around the bases of the two funnels, greatly improving the attractiveness, and indeed the usefulness of the top decks for passenger enjoyment. The funnels themselves were

*Top: The first **Queen Elizabeth** always needed tugs for manoeuvring in port as she had none of the azimuthing propulsion pods and bow thrusters of today's ships.*

*Above: The first **Queen Elizabeth** seen here towering above Southampton's Ocean Terminal in the sixties, when she and the Mary were still by far the world's largest passenger ships. (John Hendy collection).*

19

freestanding, without need of the supporting cables used in earlier ships, and there was no forward well deck, ahead of the superstructure front, also adding to the second *Queen*'s more modern appearance.

Perhaps as a result of her hasty entry into wartime service in 1940, with her commercial life only beginning some years later, or maybe merely as being the younger sister, the *Queen Elizabeth* never attracted the same media and public attention as the *Queen Mary*, though she was nonetheless a ship of equal popularity. To some extent the two *Queens* were viewed in the travelling public's eye as something of a single entity, being the veritable standard bearers of Cunard's express transatlantic service onwards through the fifties and sixties. What nobody could possibly have foreseen at the time of their design and construction during the thirties was the greatly changed modern post World War II era in which both these great liners would ultimately serve and flourish as veritable institutions through the closing decades of the liner era when travel by sea would ultimately no longer be the 'only way to cross'.

Cunard's Elizabethan Age

As Cunard had been born into, and come of age in the Victorian era, it was to be during the reign of Elizabeth II that the Line would evolve and significantly reconstitute itself into the life beat of an altogether new world of luxury leisure cruising. With the *Queen Elizabeth*'s entry into commercial service in October 1947, so began the Cunard Elizabethan era, with in its service a virtual continuum of three *Queen Elizabeth* ships. The first ship was succeeded in 1969 by the *Queen Elizabeth 2*, herself followed by the new *Queen Elizabeth* in October 2010. As part of a long-standing relationship between Cunard and the Royal Family, the first of these was launched by the late Queen Mother, HM The Queen Elizabeth at Clydebank on 27th September 1938,

with HM The Queen Elizabeth II doing the same honours for the *QE2* also on the Clyde on 21st September 1967 and naming the new *Queen Elizabeth* in Southampton on 11th October 2010.

The current Elizabethan era of the British monarchy began in 1952 when, as it was with Queen Victoria 115 years earlier, the throne passed once again to a young woman with a long and illustrious reign ahead of her. Princess Elizabeth became queen directly after her father, King George VI, died peacefully in his sleep at Sandringham House on 6th February, though the official coronation was only held on 2nd June the following year. The occasion itself already gave some insight into how times were changing. This was the first event of its kind to be televised, with an estimated 20 million viewers seeing it in their own homes or in the residences of friends, neighbours and relatives. Overseas viewers in those days, however, had to wait until copies of the film were flown to their own countries for broadcasting there, with viewers in Johannesburg receiving theirs by way of the new BOAC (British Overseas Airways Corporation) Comet airliner that had opened the jet age of air travel in May the previous year. On the other hand, there was a shortage of coachmen for Commonwealth heads of state entitled to ride in horse-drawn carriages for the coronation procession, so volunteers from various country houses and estates dressed in Palace livery engaged as stand-ins for the day.

By coronation time recovery from the ravages of war had progressed to a stage where a brightly optimistic, progressive and prosperous new age was clearly dawning in Great Britain, Western Europe, the Americas and Oceania. Despite Cold War fears of yet another occurrence of global Armageddon, South African Apartheid, and racial and social tensions around the world; the fifties and sixties brought the jet and supersonic ages in worldwide aviation, explorations into Outer Space, new pop cultures, the sexual revolution and the Baby Boom, amounting to the biggest population explosion the Western World has ever experienced. It was an era of seemingly eternal optimism that lasted well into the twentieth century's closing decades, with near full employment, steady growth in personal wealth, greater quantities of leisure time to enjoy life and more people receiving university degrees and other post-secondary-school education than ever before.

Among those passengers who were aboard the *Queen Elizabeth* on that April in 1948, Derek by then had his own general contracting business and had built a new home for Allison and the children overlooking Lake Michigan in Winnetka, just north of Chicago. Henrik and Tina had since moved further west to Washington State, while Dolfus and Lisa were working their own farmland near Bowmanville and enjoying the companionship of other families from the Netherlands who had also settled in the region, together with whom they were also building the first Rehoboth Christian Reformed Church in Canada. Meanwhile the Cunard *Queens* continued to sail heavily booked on their regular North Atlantic sailings, though already the Line was beginning to think about its options for their eventual replacement within a rapidly changing world of travel.

Ushi had found salvaging her family's hotel to be a more formidable task than she ever dreamed it would be, and by that time had succeeded only to complete the ground floor so she could reopen the restaurant and bar. From the revenue these would bring she could renovate and modernise the guest rooms piecemeal – she hoped that Meagan and Roger would be able to spend Christmas in Germany that year as her guests. Meanwhile she rewarded her modest contribution to the German *Wirtschaft Wunder* (Economic Miracle) by moving up from her dilapidated old

bicycle to a brand-new Italian Vespa. She was so excited when it arrived that she immediately rode it straight into her own bar and had a drink while still sitting astride it to the great amusement of all.

These decades also brought vast change and development throughout the entire field of transport, both passenger and cargo. Cargo shipping was being revolutionised by containerisation, supertankers and other large bulk carriers. In 1964 the 162.5 km per hour Japanese Super-Express, then the world's fastest train, was introduced in service between Tokyo and Osaka, bringing also a modern airliner-style approach in design and on-board service to the railways and setting a standard for later development of the Shinkansen bullet trains, French TGV (Trains à Grande Vitesse) and other high-speed passenger

*Above: The first **Queen Elizabeth** (top) and the Swedish America Line's new **Kungsholm**, completed in 1966 pass in opposite directions, showing the generational differences between the Cunard North Atlantic liner and the newer Swedish ship's more cruise-oriented design. (Bruce Peter collection)*

*The **United States** achieved the ultimate Blue Riband honours as the world's fastest North Atlantic liner, decisively beating the **Queen Mary**'s standing record by nearly four knots on her maiden voyage in July 1952. (FotoFlite)*

rail systems that would follow in the coming decades.[9]

Yet, perhaps the most significant transport development from a social standpoint was the ascendancy of private automobile travel. While the mass-produced Ford Model T had first made automobile ownership affordable in America as far back as 1908, the popular influence of road travel, especially in Great Britain and Europe, began to grow only after World War I. Men who were trained to operate and service motor vehicles in military service brought these skills with them as they returned to civilian life, acquiring vehicles of their own, but most importantly, building up the

needed support infrastructures for private road travel by selling petrol and other related products as well as servicing and maintaining automobiles, lorries, buses and other vehicles.[10] The introduction again of less expensive mass-produced cars such as the Volkswagen Beetle, Fiat 400 and 500 and British Motor Corporation's Mini following World War II, made the family car affordable for most households in the Western World. Traffic congestion notwithstanding, the car offered absolutely flexible personal mobility with the freedom to come and go as one pleased, with no schedules or timetables and no need to pass through terminals or *staging* points of any sort.

Car travel emerged also as a mode of transport least encumbered by social class, with everyone having the same right of way and using the same filling stations, roadside service centres and repair facilities. Even vehicles such as the Beetle and Mini had a universal appeal where they were bought as family cars by the masses and as agile and convenient *second cars* to wealthy Rolls Royce, Bentley and Mercedes Benz owners. The car has thus contributed significantly to the overall de-formalising of transport systems through the twentieth century's second half and indeed of modern society in general.

From Crossing to Cruising
Queen Elizabeth 2

The jet airliner was already capable of reducing the transatlantic crossing between London, Paris or Amsterdam to a comfortable non-stop ride of about eight hours in either direction. The crossover point, when more people were travelling by air than by sea was reached in 1958, with statistics over the following years showing too that the numbers flying were increasing more rapidly than those still sailing which were diminishing. People were beginning to travel more than ever, with a transatlantic holiday by then being possible within the two- or three-week vacation time to which most ordinary wage earners were then entitled. Cunard was faced with the huge question of what sort of ship would eventually be needed to replace the *Queens*, or even if one should be built at all. The *Queens* had already been competing since 1952 against the younger and considerably more modern American speed queen, the *United States* and the elegant new *France* completed in 1962.

Cunard's original plan was for a single 80,000-ton purebred liner code-named *Q3* (the third *Queen*-class ship) to have been ordered in 1961 and completed by 1965,

*Top: The **Queen Elizabeth 2**, then still known as Hull number 736, takes shape on the inclined ways at Clydebank. (Bruce Peter collection)*

*Above: The **Queen Elizabeth 2** is inspected by the Royal Party prior to her launching and naming by HM The Queen on 20th September 1967 as her mother had launched the old **Queen Elizabeth** from the same slipway 29 years earlier. (Bruce Peter collection)*

23

Top: The **Queen Elizabeth 2** *nearing completion in 1968 afloat at a fitting-out berth slightly downstream of where she was launched. (Bruce Peter collection)*

Above: The **Queen Elizabeth 2***, already with veranda cabins added and the Look Out lounge's forward windows gone, arriving at New York's Consolidated Passenger Ship Terminal at the end of a routine express Atlantic crossing in May 1980. (Author's photo)*

when the *Queen Mary* would be due for replacement after 30 years in service.[11] The contract was never signed as it became apparent that this was altogether the wrong approach, and that what was really needed was a smaller and more agile dual-purpose ship equally suited to both prestigious line service on the North Atlantic and luxury worldwide cruising. The idea of smaller express North Atlantic ships was in fact nothing new for Cunard, as it had been suggested at the early stages of the *Queen Elizabeth*'s planning in 1936 that a liner of about 50,000 tons would be considerably less expensive to build and more economical in operation.[12]

The unrealised *Third Queen* was succeeded by the *Q4*, in the size range of the *United States* and the then-recently completed *France*. The entire concept of this new ship, ultimately to be launched in 1967 as the *Queen Elizabeth 2*, was radically changed from an ocean liner with a gesture towards winter-season cruising to a cruise ship that would also bring a more contemporary flair to prestige transatlantic travel. She was also to be something of a destination unto herself with a wider range of facilities and services that would attract new passengers to the Atlantic during 'the season', as it was called, that ran between April and November, when the Atlantic crossing was considered to be calmer and more hospitable, and to worldwide cruising for the rest of the year. With her overall hull dimensions circumscribed to be within Panamax limits, she would be able to transit both the Panama and Suez Canals, something that the old *Queens* were unable to do.

The new ship's internal layout was radically different, with cabin spaces pushed outwards to the sides of the ship to gain the maximum number of rooms with portholes and natural light and the public areas, including the dining rooms thrust upwards for proximity to the open top decks. Fan rooms, auxiliary generators and other working areas

*The **France** completed for French Line in 1962 was a fashionably modern example of the sort of liner that Cunard's unrealised Q3 might have been if built, though probably with a more traditional style of interior design. (FotoFlite)*

that traditionally took up much of the topsides deck space aboard liners such as the old *Queens* were relegated to an unseen internal core along the ship's centreline on the lower decks. Yet in many regards the ship was also to be fairly conventional, with modern high-performance and ultra compact steam-turbine machinery placed amidships rather than fully aft, as had been done in the then recent British examples of the *Southern Cross* and *Canberra*. The superstructure, mast and funnel would, however, be made of lightweight aluminium alloy, as was done in the *United States*, *Oriana* and *Canberra*, as a weight economy measure that would allow the addition of one more deck than would otherwise have been possible.

Following the *United States*, *France*, and *Rotterdam* examples, the new Cunard ship would also bring a more modern interior design leitmotif to the North Atlantic.

*Top: The **Queen Elizabeth 2** underway sporting the light pebble grey hull colour of her post-Falklands refit that proved to be too difficult to keep clean and was soon afterwards changed back to the original dark charcoal grey. (FotoFlite)*

*Above: The **Queen Elizabeth 2** underway off the Needles after her re-engining in the winter of 1986-7 with her considerably larger diesel funnel in traditional Cunard red and black. (FotoFlite)*

Initially the Line itself had assembled a cadre of moderately progressive young British architects and designers to handle this highly prestigious commission, though as the ship was being built with Government loan guarantees, the Council of Industrial Design was eventually asked to recommend an overall design team and approach for the new ship. The sixties was a very design-aware decade when the Modern Movement was at its height and even ordinary people were buying designer furnishings and other goods for their homes, as well as wearing-apparel and other personal items from leading contemporary fashion houses.

Lord Snowdon, (Anthony Armstrong Jones), who at the time was HRH Princess Margaret's husband, was an avid advocate of modern design and a member of the Council of Industrial Design who felt that the new Cunard flagship needed to be something of a *national ship* that would appropriately represent the very best of British architectural and industrial design, graphic arts, fashion and style. Through his own support of modern design and having married into the Royal Family, Lord Snowdon was well positioned both philosophically and socially to help influence Cunard's directors to work with the Council and to accept its advice.[13] Later on, a model of the ship was shown to HM The Queen at Buckingham Palace. The Queen Mother made a private visit to architect Dennis Lennon's studio to view models and renderings of the interiors and an exhibition on the new ship at the Council of Industrial Design's showroom in London-Haymarket was opened by HRH Princess Margaret.

The *Queen Elizabeth 2* was launched by HM The Queen at Clydebank on 20th September 1967 and finally commenced her maiden voyage to New York on Friday 2nd May 1969 in what amounted to an extended weekend Atlantic crossing intended to attract those on business or holiday itineraries based on the calendar week. The *QE2's* yearly sailing schedules revolved around crossings between Southampton and New York throughout the April-to-November Atlantic season interspersed with short cruises based in Britain and the United States, with longer cruise voyages, usually including an around-the-world itinerary of which sections could be bought on an air-sea package basis, being made during the winter months. Transatlantic fly-cruise packages, with travel aboard the *QE2* in one direction and by the British Airways Concorde in the other were a very popular option during the time the delta-winged supersonic jet was in service from 1977 to 2003.

When Cunard announced the withdrawal of the venerable *Queens Mary* and *Elizabeth*, Meagan and Roger booked with Cunard for their 1967 summer holiday in America and to the Expo '67 World's Fair in Montréal that also marked Canada's centennial year. Once again they sailed out in July aboard the *Queen Mary* and back in September on the *Queen Elizabeth*'s last eastbound transatlantic crossing. Midway through the homebound crossing people began gathering on the Promenade Deck after dark for what would be the last-ever time these two great and much-loved ships would pass one another at sea. A red glow that first appeared on the eastern horizon soon revealed the *Mary*'s three red-and-black funnels brilliantly floodlit and with lights shining on deck and in just about every window and porthole as the ship steamed into full view to port side on her parallel westbound course. As the world's two greatest liners passed bridge-wing-to-bridge-wing not more than a few hundred metres one from the other the *Mary*'s three steam whistles shattered the calm of that clear autumn night with three thunderous long blasts. With the salute duly returned by the *Elizabeth*, an era in maritime history was closing, as the *Mary* herself would also be retired the following year. Meagan wiped the tears from her eyes while Roger placed his arm about her shoulders as

Top: The **Queen Elizabeth 2**'s cosy Midships Bar, inspired by its successful predecessor aboard the old Elizabeth and re-introduced as a popular gathering place aboard the new Elizabeth. (Miles Cowsill)

Above: The **Queen Elizabeth 2**'s Midships Lobby on Quarter Deck was arranged as a low podium from which passengers could make a grand entry to the first-class Columbia Restaurant (background). (Miles Cowsill)

they retired to their cabin for the night. They bought prints of both ships on board that would be suitable for framing, with an extra copy of the *Queen Elizabeth* to be taken to Germany at Christmas time for Ushi who they had met on that same stretch of deck nearly 20 years earlier.

The *Queen Mary* was bought by the City of Long Beach, California, where she has now spent more time as a tourist attraction and hotel than she did in Cunard service, and where she can still be visited and experienced today. The *Queen Elizabeth* was less fortunate. After being purchased for a similar static role in Fort Lauderdale, Florida that never materialised, she was sold again to Orient Overseas Line and sailed to Hong Kong for conversion as a floating college named the *Seawise University*, during which the ship caught fire on 9th January 1972 and heeled over onto her starboard side in Victoria Harbour the following day. The *Seawise University* was later scrapped where she lay, with part of her hull remaining on the bottom of the harbour where it now ignominiously forms part of the landfill upon which Hong Kong's Chek Lap Kok international airport was later built.

The *United States* was suddenly withdrawn from service and laid up in November 1969, followed by the *France* in September 1974, leaving the *QE2* alone for nearly four decades as the sole remaining North Atlantic express liner. The new Cunard flagship was widely acclaimed as an immediate success both in line service and cruising. Initially, she presented an amazing glimpse into the future of passenger shipping, and indeed that of Cunard itself in a new awakening from its eternally more old-world image. The *QE2* was something of an escape into space-age style, modernity and a sizeable taste of *swinging sixties* high-tech and British popular culture brought to Americana and the world as a whole. While this thrilled many, others, especially Americans, lamented its lack of the more traditional

romanticised leitmotif of things English that they had been conditioned to expect from the old *Queens*.[14]

Throughout her long and distinguished career, the *QE2* was constantly modified and refitted to keep the ship and services she offered abreast of the latest trends in cruising. Over the years her short-lived pristine modernity was gradually softened as more traditional styling elements were appliquéd over the original Formica, glass-fibre and brushed aluminium surfaces. The valances, chintzes and other purely decorative frills and curlicues that the Council of Industrial Design and original architects succeeded to keep away from the ship, gradually made their way on board over the years lending the needed sense of motherly reassuring comfortable English hominess that the original crisp modernity lacked. Yet some parts of the ship such as the elegant Queen's Room and the intimate One Deck cocktail bar that once provided discrete access to the original Princess Grill restaurant survived seemingly eternally, while the fashionable art gallery and the forward-facing Look Out lounge disappeared altogether and the Grand Lounge, originally the Double Room with its spectacular semi-circular staircase clad in glass and stainless steel, were modified beyond recognition. The *QE2* nonetheless achieved a singularly unique iconic standing throughout the world, and for Cunard was a pivotal element in the Line's own evolution from its liner background into the field of modern international luxury cruising.

The *QE2* cruised to every corner of the world, and was among the first Western cruise ships to venture into the Black Sea for calls at the Soviet ports of Odessa and Sochi. Perhaps most remarkably, she was also called to National Service for use as a troop ship during the Falkland Islands conflict with Argentina in 1982, as the old *Queens* had done during World War II, though the *QE2* made but one voyage to South Georgia Island. As her departure for the South Atlantic was being shown on German television, Ushi, by then white haired and bespectacled, glanced over her bifocals at the TV set in the hotel lobby and said, 'Haben wir alle nicht genug von Saldaten und Krieg gesehen (Haven't we all seen enough of soldiers and wars)?' The couple who were registering at the time were a former American GI named Richard from the Greater Chicago area, who had been stationed at Lahr, where he had met his bride, Astrid and since settled with her in West Germany. Looking up from the registration card he was filling in he spotted the framed print of the *Queen Elizabeth* hanging on the wall behind the front desk, and commented to Ushi that he had gone to America as a baby aboard that ship in 1948. She smiled and said that it had brought her home to Germany after the War that same year. These two people of divergent generations, nationality and backgrounds had no way of knowing how closely their life paths had passed all those years ago. Perhaps even they had literally passed 'like ships in the night' in sleeping cars on New York Central Railroad's east- and westbound *20th Century Limited* trains somewhere just east of Buffalo in Upstate New York.

Cunard's ownership changed hands several times during the *QE2*'s career, bringing other changes and influences to the Line's directorate, structure and business approach. The company was absorbed into the British-based Trafalgar House group in 1971, later passing into the hands of the Norwegian Kvaerner group as part of their overall acquisition of Trafalgar House in 1996. Neither company succeeded in being able to expand Cunard beyond being a virtually single-ship operation centred upon the *QE2*'s unique persona and sphere of operation still as a dual-role Atlantic express liner and cruise ship. While the former Norwegian America *Vistafjord* was placed under the Cunard house flag as the *Caronia*, she was but a smaller and in some ways more exclusive, second runner to the *QE2* in much the same way that the earlier Cunard *Caronia* of 1949 was never intended to be in the same league as the old *Queens*, nor was she ever regarded as such.

At the time of the Kvaerner takeover, the *QE2* was already approaching 30 years in service and despite her numerous refits, reconfiguration and refurbishment, as well as a significant life-extending re-engining with new diesel-electric machinery over the winter of 1986-7, she was becoming increasingly dated in ways that could never be overcome. The whole approach to passenger ship design had changed significantly, as had the on-board lifestyles and service expectations of those who would sail aboard them. In this regard the still highly popular and much-loved *QE2* found herself in somewhat the same position the old *Queens* were in during the sixties; still structurally and technologically sound though gradually becoming irremediably dated socially in terms of accommodations and services.

What the line really needed was a substantial fleet expansion with multiple new ships that could compete more directly with other premiere cruise lines that are also descended from the liner era such as P&O / Princess Cruises, Holland America and Costa, all of which had already built up substantial fleets of new ships. For Cunard this solution was ultimately to come out of its 1998 acquisition by Carnival Corporation, where it would find itself in the company of old friends and rivals, namely Holland America and Costa, and later on Princess Cruises and P&O and in the hands of shipping industry owners ever eager to build and expand.

The Carnival touch

As the world's biggest and most progressive cruise conglomerate Carnival has a very structured and effective approach to its considerable ship and fleet building activities – seldom does Carnival ever build just one of anything. Ships are built by series for each of Carnival's different product lines. The 100,000-ton-plus Destiny series that originated with the *Carnival Destiny* and *Triumph* in 1996-9 and six additional ships of the slightly larger *Carnival Conquest* series that followed from 2002 to 2008 became the platform for Carnival's own mass-market core Fun Ship product. The smaller Panamax-max *Spirit* class was built to offer the same features in a size able to transit the Panama Canal with the *Carnival Spirit* and three sister ships going to Carnival Cruises and the *Costa Atlantica* and *Mediterranea* to Costa. The design of each ship class is adaptable to the specific needs of one or other cruise line or product in the Carnival group, though all adopt the same technical design, engineering, propulsion and other equipment so that servicing and staffing is to some degree interchangeable across the board.

All of these are modern ships with their principal public rooms located within the hull and sleeping accommodations arranged throughout the superstructure decks so as to provide the highest possible proportion of hotel-style rooms with outside exposures and, above all, private verandas. This approach had originated in 1985 with Princess Cruises ship, the *Royal Princess* and had hitherto been repeated on but a few other upscale ships such as the second *Royal Viking Sun*, the *Crystal Serenade* and *Crystal Symphony*. Royal Caribbean's *Vision*-class *Legend of the Seas* and the *Carnival Destiny* revolutionised the cruise industry by bringing this initially rather exclusive approach directly into the mainstream market on a prodigiously large scale.

The *Vista* class was developed for the more upscale standard of the Holland America subsidiary, with the *Zuiderdam* delivered in 2002 as the first of an initial order for five ships in this series. At about the same size as the *Spirit* class, the *Vista* ships would, however, carry fewer passengers in larger cabins and suites and with a greater range of public facilities, according them a greater level of luxury and exclusivity. Newcomer Cunard's cruise fleet would ultimately be built on a lengthened and modified variant of the *Vista* class with the one exception of a single full-fledged express liner to be built as the eventual successor to the *QE2*. With the exception of their first new ship, the *Tropicale*, delivered in 1981, the *Queen Mary 2* as this ship would be named, would at least so far, be the only one-off job.

As a cruise ship, the *QM2* would be expected to offer a very high standard of predominantly veranda accommodation, a spectacular atrium and other large and spectacular public rooms, plenty of open deck space, pools, lidos and other recreational amenities, while as an express transatlantic liner she would also have to match the *QE2*'s structural stamina, power and speed. One thing that a transatlantic liner needs apart from a structurally robust hull and powerful machinery is a greater freeboard height to keep the open decks, including the cabin verandas well above the long swells and high waves that prevail on this all-too-often notoriously stormy and rough body of water.

Where Cunard had used the *QE2* as a logical starting point for the new liner's design, with the hopes of building something only slightly larger at around 80,000 to 90,000 tons, the reality of planning for a modern ship with the needed freeboard height to the boat and veranda decks, and with a higher location of the lifeboats than is prescribed by the classification societies such as Lloyd's for cruise ships, the new liner started to emerge as a considerably larger ship. With this came the domino effect of the passenger capacity being increased to make the larger size commercially viable. Cunard once again found itself building the world's largest ship as it had done with the old

Queens back in the 1930s. At 151,000 tons this was almost double the measure of the 80,000-ton *Queen Mary* and *Queen Elizabeth*.

With a ship of such great size the opportunity was taken to include a wide variety of special features including an axial layout of the principal public rooms around broad central promenades following the ship's centreline of the two main public decks. The public spaces themselves included a spectacular triple-height main restaurant and the world's first, and so far only, fully functional ocean-going planetarium, with a retractable dome allowing the room to also be used as an auditorium or cinema. In addition to the usual range of veranda cabins and suites, the sleeping accommodations included eight large duplex suites with double-height panoramic windows overlooking the stern of the ship, and an additional four single-level suites forward that can be combined into a vast single Royal Suite with its own private enclosed promenade wrapped around the front of the superstructure two decks below the navigating bridge.

Built in France by Chantiers de l'Atlantique, the *Queen Mary 2* was delivered in December 2003 and was the second Cunard *Queen* to be named by HM The Queen Elizabeth II, accompanied by HRH Philip, The Duke of Edinburgh, on 8th January 2004 at a gala celebration in Southampton. Thirty-seven years had passed since the Queen had launched the *QE2* at Clydebank. Then the ceremony was a traditional launching when the unfinished ship was slid into the water for the first time before being moved to a fitting-out berth for her completion. This time the ship was complete and ready to begin her service life. A new age had dawned in Cunard's 164-year history as the Line's first ship of the twenty-first century made her debut.

*Top: The **Queen Elizabeth 2** has, despite the numerous small changes to her exterior profile, retained a unique stance with a modern technical look and a remarkable aesthetic of form and function that have given her a truly iconic persona. (Tony Rive)*

*Above: The **Queen Elizabeth 2** again seen later in her career cruising in home waters on her last visit to the Clyde. (Miles Cowsill)*

CHAPTER 2

CREATING THE NEW
QUEEN ELIZABETH

CUNARD

QUEEN ELIZABETH

Even as the new *Queen Mary 2* made her way down Southampton Water on 12th January 2004 at the outset of her maiden voyage on an Atlantic crossing to Fort Lauderdale, Florida, the fourth *Vista*-series hull was already earmarked to go to Cunard as a cruising fleet mate to the *QM2*. As service experience was gained with the *QM2* it was decided that more time was needed to integrate what was being learned from this into the new ship, and that perhaps too it would need to be a little larger, with the fourth *Vista* ship being transferred to P&O, and recently absorbed into the Carnival group to become their new *Arcadia*. The *Queen Victoria* was the first of six slightly longer additional *Vista* ships ordered by Carnival on a piecemeal basis between 2005 and 2007, with the *Queen Elizabeth* ending the series. The remaining four ships were allotted two each to Holland America and to Costa, as that Line's first *Vistas*.

Carnival is careful to maintain the individual identities and cultures of its different cruise lines, while achieving a high level of rational consistency behind the scenes in the day-to-day operation and internal workings of its fleets. Quite apart from their distinctive latter-years *QE2*-style red and black Cunard funnels and dark charcoal grey hulls, the Cunard *Queen Victoria* and *Queen Elizabeth* are immediately discernable from the other *Vista* ships for their absence of the glassed-in panoramic lift enclosures amidships through the veranda accommodation decks, giving them a more linear ocean-liner look. While this is also a feature of the *Vista*-class *Costa Luminosa* and *Costa Delizioso*, these have white hulls, a quite different arrangement of their upper decks and Costa's current trademark minimalist stovepipe funnels giving these an altogether somewhat different look. Beyond what the eye can discern, the two Cunard ships have the additional hull strengthening, qualifying them as capable of liner service as needed for occasional

Top: The **Queen Mary 2**, *delivered to Cunard at the end of 2003 then as the world's largest passenger ship, is a remarkable combination of the express ocean liner and the upscale cruise ship with a predominance of veranda cabins. (Andrew Cooke)*

Above: The **Queen Victoria** *joined the* **QM2** *four years later as a liner-service-capable luxury cruise ship for worldwide service as a compatible fleet mate to the* **QM2**. *(Andrew Cooke)*

*Top: The **Queen Victoria** introduces a more traditional interior design approach than was adopted for the **QM2**, as seen here in the Todd English alternative-dining restaurant. (Mike Louagie)*

*Above: The **Queen Victoria** likewise presents a more traditional approach to Cunard's signature Chart Room bar, first introduced aboard the **QE2** and repeated aboard the **QM2**. (Mike Louagie)*

transatlantic crossings and other long ocean passages at a speed of 21 knots, albeit without the additional speed, exceptional seakeeping characteristics and structural might of the *QM2*.

On board, the layout and architectural design of all passenger-accessible parts of each ship are tailor made to suit the needs of each cruise line in the Carnival group and are further customised to the character of the ship individually. As sister ships, the *Queen Victoria* and *Queen Elizabeth* are of a nearly identical layout with a consistent architectural design and decorative style throughout both ships. These do, however, differ from the *QM2* which is of a somewhat different layout and a less traditional architectural and decorative style. The overall decorative palette of the *Elizabeth* is a little lighter and brighter than that of the *Victoria* in much the same way that the original *Elizabeth* was slightly more open and minimalist than the *Mary*.

The style of design for both the *Queen Victoria* and *Queen Elizabeth* makes only limited direct reference to specific places ashore or aboard other ships past or present, but is carefully devised rather to assert an overall ambience that conveys the right sense of place and occasion in a traditional context, though expressed in terms of modern-day lifestyles and service expectations. The idea is to bring forward from liners such as the original Cunard *Queens* and from the later *QE2* those features and on-board spaces that have set trends in cruising and been most influential in asserting the hallmark features of today's ships and the contemporary lifestyles now lived aboard them.

The Midships Bar introduced aboard the old *Queen Elizabeth* in place of the original ballroom as part of her adaptation for sixties-era cruising, since became a feature of the *QE2* and is now restyled in the more traditional context of the new *Victoria* and *Elizabeth*. Likewise the forward-

*The three Cunard Elizabeths including the first **Queen Elizabeth** completed in 1940, the **Queen Elizabeth 2** which made her maiden voyage in April 1969 and an early rendition before being modified of the new **Queen Elizabeth** delivered in 2010. (Courtesy of the Fincantieri collection)*

Top: The first steel is cut for fabrication of the hull and superstructure blocks in September 2008. (Brian David Smith)

Above: A section of deck is welded upside-down for ease of assembly in one of the shipyard fabrication shops before being righted and attached to one of the ship's building blocks. (Brian David Smith)

Right: A 364-ton midships lower hull block is prepared and lowered into the building dock at Monfalcone for the keel laying ceremony on 6th July 2009. (Brian David Smith)

Above left: Monfalcone Shipyard Director Paulo Capobianco poses for the camera with Cunard's then President and Managing Director Carol Marlow and shipyard chaplain Padre Gildo after the keel laying. (Brian David Smith)

Above: An upper hull block is ready for lowering into the building dock, with its large windows at its top level and one of the inset bollards for securing launches while tendering at cruise ports already in place. (Brian David Smith)

Left: A superstructure block for the veranda cabin decks above also awaits its turn to be positioned as the ship is assembled. (Brian David Smith)

37

A large key section of the lower hull housing the forward engine room, with much of the machinery already in place under protective plastic covering, is attached further astern as assembly continues after the keel laying. (Brian David Smith)

facing cocktail bars with their outlook over the bows of the original *Queens Mary* and *Elizabeth* were a source of inspiration for the Commodore Lounges aboard all three of today's Cunard *Queens*. The Verandah Grills, overlooking the after decks of the old *Mary* and *Elizabeth*, that offered exclusive alternative dining and entertainment to first-class passengers are the inspiration their inspired reinvention aboard the new *Queen Elizabeth*.

While the *QE2*'s accommodations and formal entertainment facilities have become dated for the lack of veranda cabins and suites and full-production theatres and cabaret lounges, the ship has nonetheless introduced many signature Cunard features, such as the Queen's Room with its elegant black-and-white ballroom dancing, the Yacht Club lounge for light evening entertainment, and the deluxe *Grills*-class service for occupants of the ship's top-grade suites with exclusive access to the Queen's and Princess Grill restaurants that are very much part of today's Cunard cruise experience. Against the great value of this background it becomes unnecessary and even inappropriate to try revivalist reproductions of whole interiors from the old *Queen Elizabeth* that made her last voyage more than 40 years ago. Since then as with the whole nature, geometry and structure of shipboard interiors today, the lighting, colour schemes, materials, finishes and the way in which they are used is now so radically different.

To assert a sense of the times in which ships such as the old *Queens* ruled the North Atlantic, the idea now is instead to make use of artefacts such as paintings and other graphic material, ephemera and memorabilia to make specific historical references as is Cunard's forte since a Heritage Trail was first introduced aboard the *QE2* as part of a major refit done in 1994. Building further upon the Heritage Trail idea, historical material aboard the *Queen Elizabeth* forms a more integral part of the ship's architectural and

Top: More sections are added farther astern towards the aft engine room, with some of its auxiliary equipment already in place as can be seen in the compartment to the lower left. (Brian David Smith)

Above: Looking very much like a small modern Mediterranean resort hotel under construction, one of the upper midships cabin blocks waits beside the dry dock to be lifted in place aboard the ship. (Brian David Smith)

*By September 2009 enough of the **Queen Elizabeth**'s mid section is in place that she is already starting to become recognisable as a substantial beginning of a new Cunard Queen-class ship. (Brian David Smith)*

Both sides of the forward hull sections lowered into the building dock in September 2009 are already converging to form part of the Queen Elizabeth's bow, while the superstructure blocks tower above. (Brian David Smith)

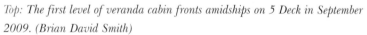

Top: The first level of veranda cabin fronts amidships on 5 Deck in September 2009. (Brian David Smith)

Top right: Inside the superstructure where these cabins will later be assembled and fitted out. (Brian David Smith)

Above and right: Scaffolding and other temporary structures inside the bare steelwork of the double-height public spaces on 2 and 3 Decks. (Brian David Smith)

Top left and left: One of the lower stern-most hull blocks is manoeuvred into position as building continues aft towards the seaward end of the building dock. (Brian David Smith)

Above: Part of the ship's steel accommodation 'hotel block' shell as it appeared in September 2009. (Brian David Smith)

Night time in early January 2010 as the ship appeared in the days immediately before her float out. (Brian David Smith)

decorative theme. The scope of this material is also extended to convey more of a general nautical theme of Cunard's place in the maritime world and to celebrate Cunard's links with the Royal Family that go back to the times of the old *Queens*. It is also extended with new original works of art created to carry a similar leitmotif.

One of the few specific architectural references on both the *Victoria* and *Elizabeth* is the Grand Lobby's staircase inspired by photographs of the grand staircase connecting the promenade- and boat-deck entrance foyers aboard White Star's *Olympic*, the world's largest liner at the time of her completion in 1911. While this is a key focal point of the Grand Lobby aboard the two ships, the spaces as a whole are neither confined to the Edwardian styling of this nor do they endeavour to be recreations of the earlier ship's foyer. The space as a whole is more generally intended rather to assert the right first impression of the new ships, what they have to offer and of the voyage that lies ahead as passengers embark, and during the voyage as a focal point for orientation to the main suites of public rooms and social contact for the time one is aboard.

A main artistic focal point of the *Queen Victoria*'s Grand Lobby is the two-and-a-half deck high bronze bas relief of the ship on a globe with a compass rose by John McKenna that recalls a similar work by the same artist in the *QM2*'s atrium, both pieces drawing their original inspiration from the famous MacDonald Gill art deco mural that remains to this day at Long Beach, California in the old *Queen Mary*'s first-class dining room. The *Queen Elizabeth*'s Grand Lobby is adorned with a charming marquetry panel of similar size depicting the old *QE* created by the celebrity furniture designer and marquetry artist Viscount Linley. Known professionally as David Linley, he is the son of Anthony Armstrong Jones, Lord Snowdon, and HRH Princess Margaret, Countess of Snowdon and sister of HM Queen

Top: On a cold and rainy day in January 2010, Monfalcone Shipyard Director Paulo Capobianco, the ship's Madrina Dennie Farmer and Cunard's new President and Managing Director Peter Shanks arrive at the dry dock for the ceremonies. (Brian David Smith)

Above: Shipyard chaplain Padre Gildo blesses the ship at the beginning of the ceremonies. (Brian David Smith)

A close-up night view looking forward along the ship's floodlit port side showing the illuminated star on her funnel from her Christmas season at Monfalcone and the temporary towers bringing various lines and hoses needed for work being done on the upper decks. (Brian David Smith)

A night view down to the bridge, superstructure front and the ship's bulbous forefoot during one of the final nights she spent in dry dock before being floated out. (Brian David Smith)

Top: Salt water from the Adriatic Sea that will lift the ship free of the blocks under her hull some hours later starts pouring into the dry dock. (Brian David Smith)

Above and right: Night views of the ship ready to be floated out the following day. (Brian David Smith)

Above left: The port side azimuthing propulsion pod, one of two that will power the ship with the propeller at its forward end. (Brian David Smith)

Above: A view of the ship's bulbous bow looking up from the bottom of the dry dock. (Brian David Smith)

Left: The huge rolling gantry crane that has lifted the ship block by block into the building dock for assembly straddles her structurally complete superstructure and funnel. (Brian David Smith)

The processional double staircase inside the Britannia Restaurant's entrance, where fair ladies in long gowns will make their grand descent to dinner on formal nights, is surrounded by scaffolding in January 2010. (Brian David Smith)

Elizabeth II. Marquetry, which traces its origins to sixteenth-century Florence, is the art of creating pictorial panels in small pieces of veneer inlaid onto a flat structural surface. Linley's 5.6 metre (18.5 foot) tall panel, showing a dramatic water level bow quarter depiction of the ship against a stylised art deco map of the Atlantic Ocean is created using the inlay of nine veneers in differing hues, including Madrona, Indian ebony, American walnut, grey ripple sycamore, burr ash, bird's eye maple, satin walnut, ash, burr walnut and Macassar ebony on a rich Vavona burr backplane.

It was felt that wood is a very British medium for such a work and that its natural lustre and warmth has a special significance in Cunard's background as veneers were used extensively throughout the interiors of the old *Queens*, particularly the *Elizabeth*, and many of the Line's other earlier ships. The old *Queen Elizabeth*'s interiors were less artsy than those of the *Mary* to the point of appearing more minimalist and contemporary, with marquetry and other special woodworking techniques being widely used to achieve the needed artistic flourish.

The Grand Lobby will also be graced with an officially commissioned portrait of The Queen who named the ship at a gala inaugural celebration in Southampton on 11th October 2010. The painting is the work of Isobel Peachey, a young Lancashire-born portrait artist who was winner of the 2009 BP Portrait Award for her striking painting in oils simply entitled *Ruth*, showing a childhood friend from the village where she grew up captured in a moment of pensiveness.[15] Cunard wanted a young artist who had never before been commissioned to paint a Royal portrait, and chose Isobel after seeing her award-winning work at the National Portrait Gallery in 2009. Isobel was granted three sittings by The Queen at Buckingham Palace for the portrait. Having no studio of her own, however, Isobel

Top: Filled with rolls of cable, construction materials, tools and other shipyard items in January 2010, the aft lido deck will be the scene of elegant country house garden parties after the ship is completed. (Brian David Smith)

Above: With rolls of cable dangling overhead and illuminated only by temporary work lamps, the double-height Royal Arcade is still but a bare steel shell in early 2010. (Brian David Smith)

51

Top: The Britannia Restaurant, fully enclosed, with glass in its panoramic windows across the ship's stern awaits its interior fitting out and furnishings. (Brian David Smith)

Above: A close-up view of the ship's port side amidships with the nearly completed Grills restaurants housing in place. (Brian David Smith)

Right: With their dividing partitions yet to be installed, though with temporary safety railings in place, the cabin verandas provide an alternative route for shipyard workers to move about the ship. (Brian David Smith)

completed the painting in the attic of her mother's home.

The portrait shows a charming softly lighted three-quarters view of The Queen seated in Buckingham Palace's Yellow Drawing Room, dressed in pale blue and wearing the necklace and earrings from Queen Victoria that she wore for her coronation in 1953. The work was unveiled at a private function in the National Portrait Gallery in London on Monday 20th September 2010 without being publicly displayed at the Gallery prior to being hung aboard the *Queen Elizabeth*.

The Queen's Room is decorated with murals showing views from various British royal palaces and also displays the Royal Standard presented to the old *Queen Elizabeth* by the Queen Mother when she launched the ship in 1938. The Queen's Room also has a display of framed photographs from Cunard's Royal ship launchings and naming ceremonies as well as of the numerous visits members of the Royal Family have made to the Line's ships over the years.

A globe in the ship's library shows the world as it was in the 1930s when the old *Queens* were built and there are large models of Cunard liners prominently displayed in a number of the public rooms, including the Yacht Club, Commodore Club and the Midships Bar. The *Queen Elizabeth*'s two Grand Suites and Four Master Suites are named after the six Cunard Commodores, Sir James Bisset, Sir Edgar Britton, Sir James Charles, Sir Cyril Illngworth, Sir Arthur Rostron and Sir Ivan Thompson, who were knighted over the years. A framed portrait photo and thumbnail biography for each of these is displayed in the suite named in his honour.

There are a number of architectural differences between the *Queens Victoria* and *Elizabeth* that to some extent no doubt reflect initial service experience with the *Victoria*, but that nonetheless serve to further assert the individuality of

Top: Moored at a pier for the completion of fitting-out and interior work, the **Queen Elizabeth** *begins to take on a far more completed look by April 2010. (Brian David Smith)*

Above: By this time uptakes and other funnel fittings are completed. (Brian David Smith)

53

each ship. Outwardly, the aft terracing of the upper cabin decks of the *Queen Elizabeth* is shortened, adding space for some additional veranda cabins and extending the open lido deck further astern. The same modification was also made in Costa and Holland America's latest *Vista* ships The *Queen Elizabeth*'s forward Games Deck above the bridge is given a higher surrounding windscreen wall to support a canvas canopy above the bowls green that is added here.

There are also a number of differences in the on-board spaces of these two newest Cunard *Queens*. The *Victoria*'s Hemispheres, with its 270-degrees of wrap-around windows overlooking the midships pool and lido decks, becomes a new adaptation of the *QE2*'s Yacht Club lounge, picking up the lively evening atmosphere of its namesake added in one of the mid-life refits of the earlier ship, while also retaining flexibility to be used for other daytime activities including business meetings, conferences and private events.

The *Victoria*'s Winter Garden becomes the Garden Lounge adjacent to the *Elizabeth*'s Pavilion Pool, where it has been given a semi-circular domed roof, creating a seagoing impression of the Glass Houses at London's Kew Gardens as a conservatory lounge complete with tall potted palms and other foliage. There is a greater separation of this Garden Lounge's air-conditioned interior from the Pavilion Pool and other outside areas thanks to the thoughtful addition of double inner and outer automatic sliding glass doors that in effect provide an airlock between the inside and outside areas. A supper club service is offered in this area, providing an added alternative dining venue aboard the *Elizabeth* where light dinner selections

*Left: The **Queen Elizabeth**'s outboard starboard side shows progress with the fold-down tender landing stages fitted along B Deck and painting of the hull in progress. (Brian David Smith)*

Top: A distant glimpse over the lovely Italian countryside near Monfalcone from the yet-to-be glazed Commodore Club windows high above the ship's bridge. (Brian David Smith)

Above: In April 2010 the Britannia Restaurant stairway is still awaiting its completion. (Brian David Smith)

Right: At the same time, however, work is in progress on the Carinthia Club's decorative ceiling panels. (Brian David Smith)

Above left: With its oak banisters under protective covering, the Grand Staircase is amidst considerable fitting-out activity, impassable beneath scaffolding and draped with a shipyard services hose. (Brian David Smith)

*Above: As work continues on the **Queen Elizabeth**'s exterior the Garden Lounge's glass roof is already in place as seen to the left of the temporary shipyard ventilation tower. (Brian David Smith)*

Left: By April most of the shipyard material has been cleared from the aft lido deck though it still awaits completion. (Brian David Smith)

57

Top: The Queen's Room is temporarily decked over with scaffolding at its mezzanine level on 3 Deck as work continues on its finished ceiling and lighting fixtures. (Brian David Smith)

Above: The Royal Court Theatre's private boxes begin to appear amidst a veritable forest of scaffolding and other temporary fixtures. (Brian David Smith)

Right: Topsides work continues on the Pavilion Pool and Lido beneath a protective canopy with the three-quarters circular Yacht Club glass enclosure and dome taking shape in the background. (Brian David Smith)

from a *taster's menu* can be enjoyed with dancing and other entertainment. To some degree this also draws upon Carnival's extensive and diverse building experience, where the Cunard Garden Lounge dome can be seen as a refinement and more exclusive treatment of similar glass canopies worked into the forward part of the funnel base aboard the *Carnival Spirit* ships earlier in the decade.

Owing to the great popularity of the Café Carinthia, introduced aboard the *Victoria*, its counterpart aboard the *Elizabeth* is extended into space that in the earlier ship was occupied by a separate Champagne Bar. Where the Chart Room Bar, a feature first introduced aboard the *QE2*, is adjacent to the main Britannia Restaurant's lower-level main entrance aboard the *Victoria*, the corresponding space in the *Elizabeth* is occupied by the newly introduced Britannia Club. This is a club-style alternative restaurant with open seating and flexible meal times for passengers in upper-grade veranda accommodations. Its function is similar to that of the Caronia Restaurant introduced as part of the *QE2*'s major refit in 1994, when the ship's dining arrangements were vastly rearranged with the original Upper Deck Britannia Restaurant being reworked into a more intimate scale to serve passengers in the higher-grade cabins.

The entrance to the new *Queen Elizabeth*'s main Britannia Restaurant is reworked with the twin circular staircases off to either side of its entrance foyer aboard the *Victoria* replaced by a single processional stairway descending from its upper to lower level directly from the forward end of the room's double-height nave. This provides for ladies in their long gowns to make a theatrical *grand descent*, from on high as they would have done aboard the *Ile de France* and *Normandie* at dinner time on formal evenings. This was something that was never possible aboard the old Cunard Queens since, as grand as their first-class dining rooms were,

Top: A photorealistic digital rendering of the Garden Lounge gives a foretaste of this charming room's reference to the Glass Houses of London's Kew Gardens. (Cunard)

Above: The Verandah Restaurant's interior as shown in this photorealistic digital rendering will be the place on board that is most evocative of the old **Queen Elizabeth** *interior architecture. (Cunard)*

Top: The Library interior starts to take shape in July 2010 as wall and ceiling coverings begin to go into place.(Brian David Smith)

Above: Servery cabinets are installed in the main galley with protective covering to keep these in pristine condition as other work continues around them. (Brian David Smith)

*Right: The large niche with its Romanesque arch above the Grand Staircase is ready for the Linley marquetry panel depicting the old **Queen Elizabeth** that will grace the Grand Lobby. (Brian David Smith)*

Top left: Work continues on the Britannia Restaurant, as lighting fixtures and wall coverings go into place around the room's central double-height axis. (Brian David Smith)

*Left: One of the **Queen Elizabeth**'s large catamaran excursion launches is already in its davits above the Promenade Deck. (Brian David Smith)*

Above: With shop fronts still to be completed, balustrades and banisters fitted, the Royal Arcade begins to take on its finished appearance as illustrated in the architects' renderings. (Brian David Smith)

61

they were entered directly at floor level from the foyer. The gesture was, however, made aboard the *QE2* where her original first-class Columbia Restaurant was entered from a small raised podium incorporated into the adjacent deck lobby.

The original Verandah Grills from the old *Queens* are reborn as The Verandah Restaurant created in the space that is occupied by the Todd English alternative dining venue aboard the *Victoria*. The Verandah interior is designed in a stunning art deco style, with murals and art pieces that reflect the joyous and whimsical leitmotif of the originals nearly 75 years ago. The scheme is altogether new with brighter lighting and a more modern service approach. The effect is achieved without endeavouring to do a revivalist treatment of the old Verandah Grills, though it nonetheless does capture an impression of the ambience of these in which film stars, sport celebrities, business tycoons and other celebrities of the day dined, mingled and were entertained in great luxury. Among these were Hollywood film stars such as Clark Gable and Rita Hayworth, and the Duke and Duchess of Windsor following the Duke's controversial 1936 abdication of the throne terminating his reign of only 325 days as King Edward VIII. Carefully researched and created by Cunard's Corporate Executive Chef and global culinary ambassador, Strasbourg-born Jean-Marie Zimmermann, responsible for the gastronomy aboard all three of today's *Queens*, the Verandah menus offer a faithful recreation of the gastronomy that was enjoyed in the original Verandah Grills as well as contemporary French and international cuisine.

All gastronomy throughout the Cunard fleet, from the haute cuisine of the Queen's and Princess Grills and other exclusive alternative restaurants or indeed of the main Britannia Restaurant, right down to the *gateaux* and *petit*

fours served at teatime in the Queen's Room, the *bangers and mash* dished up to thirsty patrons in the Golden Lion Pub and cabin room service items delivered in the wee hours of the morning, is the ultimate responsibility of Executive Chef Zimmermann. He, and his high standards of gastronomy and its presentation, are in effect represented by some two hundred Chefs, Sous-Chefs, Bakers, Confectioners, Maitre D's, Sommeliers, Stewards, Stewardesses, Busboys, Dishwashers and Scullery Hands aboard each of the three Cunard *Queens*. The overall style and presentation of food service throughout the Cunard fleet is an interpretative form of classic modern gastronomy that appeals to the broader cross-section of today's younger passengers and adapts to the inclusion of various national and regional specialties to be expected on world cruises and other longer voyages.

There is an increasingly strong emphasis on alternative dining, with each of Cunard's new *Queens* having its own unique dining experiences such as the *Elizabeth*'s Verandah Grill and new Supper Club dining options in the Café Carinthia and Garden Lounge, for which individual specialised menus are prepared. Cruise passengers are also more inclined to try new and regional cuisines aboard ship when they feel confident about the quality of the ingredients and the craft of the cooking in the familiar settings of the ship's main and alternative restaurants.

Top-quality ingredients are, of course, a key aspect of gastronomy such as this, and while the ship is provisioned in Great Britain and the United States for periods of up to three months, fresh meats, produce, dairy products, and other items are taken on board regularly. Provision is also made for various specialty items from around the world to be acquired locally during world cruises and other long voyages and even for the purchase of fresh produce, sea foods and other specialties from reliable sources at various

By April 2010 the Golden Lion Pub is but roughed in and separated from the adjacent Royal Court by the white steel bulkhead with its line of openings (but will soon hold many of the pub's Tudor-style windows). (Peter David Smith)

Top: Outfitting and equipping of the Royal Court Theatre is already well advanced with the private boxes in place, the auditorium lighting operational and work on the stage itself, with its scenery handling and other production facilities being installed and tested. (Brian David Smith)

Above: Work inside the Grills Lounge continues behind the protective coverings over its panoramic windows and glass dome. (Brian David Smith)

ports of call for 'catch of the day' and 'farm to table' offerings in menus of the day. In the luxury dining experience in a fine restaurant or hotel ashore, or aboard a ship such as the *Queen Elizabeth*, the presentation is as important as are the recipes, ingredients, preparation and service. The gastronomy is carefully prepared and served to look as appetising as it tastes, as its visual presentation has first to be appealing to the eye so that it will excite the palate.

Shopping has always been a special attraction aboard the Cunard *Queens*, where well-known British High Street shops such as W. H. Smith & Son booksellers and department store Austin Reed of London were first introduced aboard the *Queen Mary* in 1936, following French Line's lead of commissioning a small ocean-going branch of the Paris department store Les Galleries Lafayette aboard the *Normandie* the previous year. As shopping facilities were expanded aboard the *QE2* during the eighties, ocean-going branches of Harrods, Bally Leather Goods and Alfred Dunhill were added as these and other retailers also expanded into airport shopping with tax-free outlets in the international terminals at London Heathrow, Amsterdam-Schiphol, Paris-Charles de Gaulle and others.

In addition to the many brands already familiar to Cunard passengers, the *Queen Elizabeth*'s Royal Arcade will be graced by the exclusive London department store Fortnum & Mason's first-ever premises at sea. Established in 1707 by William Fortnum, a footman to Queen Anne, and thus well connected in Court circles,[16] and by Hugh Mason who had already founded a successful grocery business in Piccadilly, this still-privately-owned business is the holder or Royal Warrants as Grocers, Confectioners, Oilmen, Furnishers and Warehousemen by appointment to the Royal Family. Fortnum's, as it is more popularly known, is still best known for its food department and is world famous for its selection of loose-leaf teas, luxury picnic hampers and other specialised foodstuffs. On board the *Queen Elizabeth* Fortnum's offers a selection of non-perishable packaged food items such as teas, preserves and confections as well as other luxury goods and gift items.

The making of Cunard's new *Queens* goes beyond merely designing and building the ship to also introducing a unique atmosphere and experience to be enjoyed on board, long remembered afterwards and an encouragement to return again to the *Queens*. In addition to the broad range of entertainment, enrichment programmes, sports and other pastimes offered on all Cunard ships, the *Queen Elizabeth* presents a special theme element based on the thirties and forties era of the original *Queens*.

A thirties-era country house weekend was chosen as the *Queen Elizabeth* theme, recalling an age when the rich and famous of the day, most of whom probably *crossed* regularly on the *Queen Mary* (the *Elizabeth* only went into service in 1947) would invite groups of their families and friends for weekend getaways to their country homes and estates. The *Queen Elizabeth* endeavours to create a perhaps charmed and romanticised impression of these fairly informal social gatherings with activities such as lawn bowling and croquet on the Games Deck above the bridge. This is set up as a traditional British bowls green and croquet lawn for these garden games that were a part of the country house weekend ashore. Country house weekend events will also include a seagoing adaptation of the traditional garden party held on the extended aft lido deck, with ladies in summer frocks and gentlemen in striped blazers and boater hats, as well as after dinner gatherings around the piano for Ivor Novello evenings in the Midships Bar. This is of course in addition to the many other traditional institutions of genteel British living such as tea dances in the Queen's Room, white-gloved afternoon tea service and a lively pub

*Top: With less than three months to go before delivery, the **Queen Elizabeth** appears to be well on her way to being completed. (Brian David Smith)*

Above: The Queen's Room's ceiling nears completion with its indirect cornice and spot lighting already working and preparation made for installation of the two chandeliers above the dance floor. (Brian David Smith)

65

life with darts tournament play, and genuine *pub grub*.

Other events related to the times of the old *Queens* include screenings of films from the thirties and forties, for which the Royal Court Theatre is also equipped as a cinema with 35mm film projectors, as well as big band and swing-era ballroom dancing. There are also dance classes for these as well as specialty dances of those times such as the Lindy Hop and Jitterbug.

The passenger travelling aboard the new *Queen Elizabeth* today has every reason to be as thrilled by the service as Allison and Derek, the two Dutch families, Ushi, Meagan and Roger, and their shipmates all were when they crossed the Atlantic on the old *Elizabeth* in the early days of her commercial career back in April 1948. As much as she fully enjoyed a happy and fulfilling life in her adopted new homeland of America, where she watched Derek's business

flourish and her children grow up, Allison still felt homesick for England at times. She had kept every single menu, daily programme, all of the photographs and even some of the baggage tags from that voyage. When Derek finally sold the contracting business in 1989, he and Allison flew to London the following May aboard the British Airways supersonic Concorde for a seven-night stay at the London Ritz, returning home by way of New York aboard the *QE2*.

Allison felt that the *QE2* itself was quite different and far more Americanised than what she still vividly recalled of the old *Elizabeth*, though she was thrilled to find that, in addition to the casino, health spa and other newer amenities, on-board living still revolved around such charming traditional institutions of gracious English living as tea dances and afternoon tea in the elegant Queen's Room and formal Black-and-White evenings of ballroom dancing. There was still that very special British sense of the way things are done and the approach to service that is always courteous, caring and thoughtfully attentive, though never intrusive, that had also made the 1948 crossing so remarkable and memorable. This time there would be no long wait in Grand Central Station, but rather a short taxi ride to La Guardia Airport for a midday flight home of little more than an hour, where Gill would be waiting at O'Hare International Airport with the car. As the Boeing 737 airliner made its landing approach over the apartment buildings along Chicago's Lake Shore Drive, the city's parklands and downtown skyscrapers, Allison gazed out over the City's familiar landmarks, realising at long last that this was now her real home.

*One of the six V-type Wärtsilä 40S Series medium-speed main diesel engines running the generators powering the **Queen Elizabeth**'s propulsion pods, bow thrusters and stabilisers as well as supplying the ship's entire on-board electrical needs. (Brian David Smith)*

*Right: A post-sea-trials view of the **Queen Elizabeth**'s upper decks from the main mast, with the Garden Lounge dome complete, plants on the Grills lido deck and even deck chairs scattered around the Pavilion Lido, though alas, no water yet in the pool. (Brian David Smith)*

CHAPTER 3

BUILDING THE QUEEN ELIZABETH

CUNARD

QUEEN ELIZABETH

As a product of today's highly consolidated and globalised shipbuilding industries, the *Queen Elizabeth* was built in Italy at the Fincantieri Monfalcone Yard on the Adriatic Sea north-west of Trieste near the Slovenian border. Officially known as Società Finanziaria Cantieri Navali – Fincantieri S.p.A. (Società per Azioni, i.e. an actively traded public company) and headquartered in Trieste, the company was originally established in 1959 as a State-backed amalgamation of Italy's shipyards. Today Fincantieri is a leader in world shipbuilding and marine engineering, having, since its creation, absorbed Italy's eight major shipyards, amassing the shipbuilding experience of some 200 years through the building of more than 7,000 ships of all types including passenger liners, cargo vessels and naval ships. Fincantieri's major centres of passenger shipbuilding activity are at Monfalcone and Marghera located in the outskirts of Venice. The company also maintains major design and technical departments at both of these locations.

Formerly Cantiere Riuniti dell Adriatico, the Monfalcone Yard has built such famous and well-known liners as Italian Line's pre-war *Conte di Savoia* and her sixties era successor *Raffaello*, along with the Home Lines' *Oceanic* and Costa's *Eugenio C*, while the Ansaldo, Sestri Ponente Yard in Marghera had built the Italian Line's 1932 Blue Riband record holder *Rex* and later the *Andria Doria* and the *Rafaello*'s sister ship *Michelangelo*. Both yards have since become major builders of today's highly sophisticated cruise ships and ferries. Monfalcone is Fincantieri's largest yard with Holland America's *Statendam* series, *Carnival Destiny / Triumph*, Princess's *Sun Princess* series and the lead ships of the *Grand Princess* class, and most recently P&O's *Ventura* and *Azura*, along with the also new *Carnival Dream* series to its credit. Meanwhile the Marghera Yard has delivered the *Costa Classica / Romantica*, the *Disney Magic / Wonder*, Holland America's 1998 *Rotterdam*, the *Amsterdam*, the second Carnival *Vista* series with the exception

Top: An aerial view of the Monfalcone Yard with Dry Dock 1, where the **Queen Elizabeth** *was built. (Fincantieri)*

Above: P&O's **Azura** *was being fitted out as seen here on the opposite side of the pier where the* **Queen Elizabeth** *was berthed for completion following her float out in January 2010. (Brian David Smith)*

*Top: The **Pride of Rotterdam**, seen here at Rotterdam, she was built for P&O's North Sea ferry services at Monfalcone in 2001. (Miles Cowsill)*

*Above: The **Carnival Magic** takes shape during the late summer of 2010 in Dry Dock 1 following the **Queen Elizabeth**'s float out earlier in the year. (Fincantieri)*

of the *Queen Elizabeth*, as well as the North Sea Ferries' *Pride of Rotterdam* and *Hull*.[17]

Carnival's long-standing relationship with Fincantieri at Monfalcone began with the four-ship *Statendam* series building, with the *Statendam* delivered in 1992. The *Costa Classica / Romantica* and the P&O *Grand Princess*, from Marghera, also during the mid nineties, were built before these Lines were later absorbed by Carnival. The *Vista* ships are in fact a larger rendition of the Monfalcone-built *Statendam* series and the slightly larger *Rotterdam* and *Amsterdam* that followed from Marghera in 1997 and 2000 respectively. The Vista series in essence expanded and adapted the original *Statendam* plan to meet the emerging new standards of luxury cruise ships featuring a predominance of veranda accommodations arranged throughout their superstructure decks. The two main runs of public spaces were lowered by two decks and inverted so that the larger full-beam rooms were on the deck beneath the lifeboats rather than above them. Drawing also from the experience of the *Carnival Spirit* design, the superstructure's mid body above was narrowed so as to gain an extra deck height without compromise of stability to provide the maximum proportion of passenger rooms with verandas.

While the original five *Vistas* were built at Monfalcone, construction of the slightly larger second series has for the most part gone to Marghera on the basis of earliest availability of a building berth at the time these were each ordered. Last of the *Vistas* (unless yet more of these are ordered later), the *Queen Elizabeth*, was booked back at Monfalcone where the first five ships and the earlier *Statendam* series were built. Thus Monfalcone and Marghera have each built one of the Cunard Queens.

*Right: The **Queen Elizabeth**'s funnel is complete and operational, with all of its uptakes topped off and the horn trumpets in place along with the ship's name boards. (Brian David Smith)*

CHAPTER 4

FROM 'THE STEEL' TO THE QUEEN

Actual building of the *Queen Elizabeth* began in September 2008 when the first steel was cut at Monfalcone. In the time that had passed since the building contract was signed in late 2007 the design work was completed and detailed working and *shop* drawings were prepared for the ship's fabrication at the Yard and for the many equipment suppliers and turnkey providers of just about everything from machinery, lifesaving equipment, and electronics systems to already completed cabins, interior fittings and furnishings. Steel and other materials for the build itself along with everything that would go into the ship were ordered and their deliveries carefully scheduled for the stages of building when they would be needed.

As the first steel is cut, construction begins in the Yard's fabrication shops with assembly of the ship as individual *blocks* that would later be assembled in the dry dock. These are several decks high, the full width of the ship, with the largest midship's so-called *grand blocks* being 32.6 metres long and weighing up to 720 tons apiece. Vertically, the lower blocks extend up from the ship's keel and double bottom to A Deck, below the passenger accommodations and atop the watertight bulkheads that subdivide the hull. The second strata tops off at the boat deck promenade level on 3 Deck, with the two tiers of main superstructure blocks above each being three decks high. The structures above these, including all of the upper-deck's public facilities, the mast and funnel form the final layer of blocks. Yet the completed ship gives no indication of having been built from blocks as its smooth welded surfaces beneath the gloss superstructure and hull paint, under the finished decks and behind the *dressed* interior surfaces gives virtually no indication of where the meticulously welded seams are located.

This approach offers the great advantage over conventional shipbuilding that most of the machinery and other heavy equipment is placed aboard the ship as the

Cunard's President and Managing Director Peter Shanks stands with Viscount Linley in front of a half-scale rendering of the Queen Elizabeth marquetry panel unveiled at Linley's London Studio in May 2010.

Top: With onlookers watching, the **Queen Elizabeth** *manoeuvres away from the pier under her own power as she commences her sea trials. (Fincantieri)*

Above: In the precautionary care of harbour tugs the nearly completed **Queen Elizabeth** *heads out to the open Adriatic Sea against a backdrop of the pleasing Italian countryside surrounding the Monfalcone Yard. (Fincantieri)*

blocks are assembled in the dry dock rather than having to be lowered down the engine casing after the superstructure is erected and the ship launched. The main diesel generator sets that weigh two-hundred-or-so tons apiece are lifted individually into the engine room blocks after they have been positioned in the dry dock and before these are covered by the structures above them. Much of the piping, cabling and ventilation ductwork and other services are already in place, needing only to be connected as the blocks are assembled in the dry dock. Complex structures such as strength decks, where structural trusses and ribs need to be welded can be assembled upside-down on the shop floor for ease of fabrication and righted as the block itself is put together.

The *Queen Elizabeth*'s keel was in effect laid when the first hull block was lowered into Dry Dock 1 on Monday 6th July 2009. The event was commemorated with a small ceremony where Cunard's then President and Managing Director Carol Marlow pressed the large red button on a device that looked like an oversized computer mouse, signalling the crane operators above to lower the 364-ton midship's lower hull module the final couple of metres onto the supporting blocks already laid out on the dock's bottom to support the ship through the following six months of her steel fabrication there. The dock had been vacated only days earlier when the *Carnival Dream* was floated out, and was already surrounded by other hull and superstructure blocks for the *Queen Elizabeth*.

The completed blocks are lowered and precisely positioned to the millimetre in the dry dock where they are arc welded together and the services already inside them connected, working from the ship's mid-body forward and aft toward the bow and stern. The two big gantry cranes that straddle the Monfalcone's Dry Dock 1 each have a lifting capacity of 400 tons, and are equipped to work in tandem to handle the heavier lifts of up to 750 tons. On the dry dock floor, scaffolding and *cherry pickers* are used to give working access to parts of the hull and superstructure as needed. Completion of passenger deck spaces, fitting out of the interior and other finishing work will only be undertaken after the ship is floated out of the dry dock and moved to a fitting-out dock. Until then the construction process is almost entirely a matter of steel fabrication. From the time the first steel was cut until the float out, the ship herself is usually referred to by shipyard people merely as 'the steel,' reflecting a special sense of pride in the Yard's prowess in its steelwork and welding that gives the ship her structure and strength.

The *Queen Elizabeth* was floated out on Tuesday 5th January 2010, with the occasion marked, first by the welding of a small steel box containing three coins set into solid Plexiglas to the Games Deck bulkhead below the mast as a symbol of good luck for the ship. The coins themselves denote the launch years of Cunard's three *Elizabeth* ships with a 1938 half crown, and sovereigns from 1967 and 2010. These were welded in place by Cunard President and Managing Director Peter Shanks and by guest of honour Mrs. Florence (Dennie) Farmer, chosen by Cunard as the new *Elizabeth*'s Madrina or Godmother. Her late husband Willie Farmer had served as Chief Engineer on both the first *Elizabeth* and the *QE2*, and since his death some years ago Dennie has sailed often aboard the Line's ships. The second stage of the ceremony was the actual float out. The Madrina was given a small axe to cut a wire releasing the bottle of Italian prosecco to shatter against the ship's side as salt water from the Adriatic Sea began to pour into the dry dock. The ceremony and celebratory luncheon that followed were long over when the *Queen Elizabeth*'s hull finally floated free from its supporting blocks some hours later under the watchful eyes of shipyard personnel supervising the event. Only eight days later the *Queen Elizabeth*'s place in Dry Dock 1 was taken with the keel laying for the *Carnival Dream*, for which the

*Top: The portrait of The Queen commissioned for the **Queen Elizabeth** is unveiled at the National Portrait Gallery in London by its artist, Isobel Peachey and a museum worker as Peter Shanks looks on. (Cunard)*

*Above: Among the many genuine Cunard and **Queen Elizabeth** artefacts displayed throughout the ship is this unusual one-piece smooth metal casting of the **QE2**. (Brian David Smith)*

diesel-generator sets, hull and superstructure blocks were already lined up beside the dock.

Once moved to the fitting-out dock for completion, where among a myriad of other things, the name was welded to both sides of the bow, the stern and the large name boards atop the superstructure, the ship began to take on more of her persona of as the *Queen Elizabeth*. Construction from this stage onwards is more akin to building ashore, though with the structure being serviced by dockside cranes on rails rather than a jack-up boom crane on the top deck. Openings in each deck and handling stages attached to the ship's side facilitate handling of larger items such as the already manufactured cabins and the interior assemblies for the larger suites and the public areas. The already largely fitted out, though at this point floorless, cabins are rolled aboard through side openings on each deck using specially-made castors with release mechanisms that allow them to be detached and removed once the module is positioned, aligned with its window openings and other structural connections and ready to be secured in place.

Plumbing, electrical and HVAC (Heating Ventilation and Air Conditioning) service runs are already in place, usually above the passageway ceiling, and need only to be connected. The great advantage of this approach is that manufacturing of the cabins and interior assemblies for the public spaces is already being carried out by the suppliers of these in their own factories ashore while the steel is being cut and fabricated into the ship's building blocks at the Yard. This greatly reduces the time span from cutting the first steel to delivering the completed ship. The first *Queen Elizabeth* took

*Left: In absolutely pristine condition, the gleaming new **Queen Elizabeth** takes final leave of her birthplace on 30th September 2010 in the late afternoon Mediterranean sun, bound for her home port of Southampton. (Brian David Smith)*

Top: The Britannia Restaurant's double curved ceremonial staircases. (Brian David Smith)

Above: A Queen's Grill-grade suite, showing the modern light and bright appearance of the ship's passenger accommodations that draws upon well-proven design experience from the original Holland America Vista-class ships. (Cunard)

about 40 months to build from the time of her keel laying to her completion compared with the 24 months from when the first hull blocks were assembled for the new *Elizabeth* until she was handed over to Cunard.

Temporary service towers are fitted at various points along the ship's sides to bring ventilation, electrical power and other services from ashore to the interiors as these are completed and their own internal services eventually brought into operation. There are also portable external stair towers forward and aft to provide quick access to all superstructure decks and serve as fire escapes in the event of an emergency. Gradually as glass is fitted in the Commodore Club windows above the bridge and in the full-height Grill Restaurants' windows, the deck railings and the supporting elements for the Games Deck canopy are added. Meanwhile, the lifeboats and excursion launches are suspended under their launching davits and so the *Queen Elizabeth* takes on a more complete and ship-shape appearance in readiness for her sea trials in the summer of 2010.

By mid June the *Queen Elizabeth*'s main engines were started for the first time and the six diesel generator sets brought on stream to the main electrical switchboard for distribution of electrical power and light throughout the ship. With this the ship began to come to life and *breathe* on her own as the deck lights come on and the public spaces, and the accommodations which are nearing completion are finally illuminated the way they will be seen when the first passengers embark four months later on in October. Air conditioning and other services can be powered and started as their installations and testing are completed while umbilical services from onshore are disconnected and removed as the ship nears completion.

At 08.44 on the morning of Friday 13th August the *Queen Elizabeth* manoeuvred away from her fitting-out berth under her own power to start three days of sea trials in the Adriatic.

*The Grand Lobby looking aft on 3 Deck towards the centrepiece Linley marquetry panel of the first **Queen Elizabeth** above the lower Grand Staircase with part of the forward upper Grand Staircases visible to the right and left of the photo. (Brian David Smith)*

Musicians take their places for the first time on the Queen's Room's stage for an orchestra rehearsal as the ship's company assembles on board during the final week before her handover and departure from Monfalcone. (Brian David Smith)

With three hundred people aboard from the shipyard, various suppliers of the machinery and other equipment, Cunard and Lloyd's Register, under whose rules the ship will be classified, the purpose of the trials was to put the *Queen Elizabeth* through her paces at sea in readiness for her delivery to Cunard some six weeks later. The trials determine that the ship meets her design specifications, including perhaps most importantly the service speed of 21.7 knots and determine the maximum trial speed, which in the *Queen Elizabeth*'s reached 24.3 knots.

The sea trials serve to test the ship's manoeuvrability, stability, rolling, incline and general sea-keeping characteristics. Turning and full-stop tests are made at full and cruising speeds and various emergency situations such as blackout conditions are exercised. The trials also provide a final opportunity for any sources of vibration and noise to be identified and remedied in the final weeks of fitting out still remaining. At this stage the ship is still the property and responsibility of her builders, with the trials thus being made under the Italian flag and a temporary Italian registry under the control of shipyard trials crew, with Cunard's officers designated aboard as observers and understudies. Catering and hotel services for the trial voyage are arranged by a local turnkey service provider, usually with everyone being fed in the crew cafeteria and berthed in already-completed staff and standard-grade passenger cabins on the lower decks.

At the conclusion of her trials on Sunday afternoon, the *Queen Elizabeth* was dry docked at Trieste for a final inspection of her hull's underside, the propulsion pods, stabilisers and bow thrusters and a thorough cleaning and final painting of all underwater surfaces in readiness for her delivery to Cunard. Once the painting was completed, the *Queen Elizabeth* moved once again to a fitting-out berth for the final completion of her interiors and a thorough cleaning ready for delivery. At this stage, the remaining Cunard crew,

The completed Royal Arcade, looking forward along the ship's centreline at its upper level on 3 Deck towards the Dent & Company Big Ben clock, with one of the Empire Casino's one-armed bandits visible at the lower left. (Brian David Smith)

*Top: The Golden Lion Pub has a more art deco approach than its counterpart aboard the **Queen Victoria**. (Brian David Smith)*

Above: Art deco decoration of the indoor Spa Pool is clearly reminiscent of the pool interiors aboard the first Queens, located as they were, deep within their hull decks. (Brian David Smith)

staff and other personnel, begin to arrive to prepare the ship for her delivery voyage to Southampton and her entry into commercial service.

At 06.00 as dawn is breaking on Friday 17th September the new *Queen Elizabeth*'s crew and company begin to arrive at the Fincantieri yard and their new ocean-going home. Those who were involved with the building and fitting out were brought from their hotels and apartments while others started arriving directly from Trieste's Friuli-Venezia Giulia airport where they were met by Cunard representatives. During the week or so before the ship's delivery voyage to Southampton they would be busy settling into their new on-board homes and getting ready for work, with duty rosters being set up and just about everything from general ship's stores to cookware, crockery and cutlery to be unpacked and put away. In the hospital, medical equipment had to be set up and tested and the dispensary stocked with the pharmaceuticals that had been delivered. The beds in just over a thousand cabins and suites would have needed to be made up, and bath linens, toiletries bath robes and slippers put out for the guests and others who would make the delivery voyage.

In the Royal Theatre stage sets, costumes and other items already loaded aboard needed to be unpacked and placed for the ship's theatre company to start rehearsing in their new *play house*. Meanwhile the orchestra was already practising in the middle of the Queen's Room's thousand-square-foot dance floor amid scaffolding and a team of shipyard workers were putting the final touches to the room's interior decoration. Grand pianos and casino *one-armed bandits* were still being lifted aboard along with moveable furnishings such as tables and chairs for the Golden Lion pub and paintings had been placed leaning against walls waiting to be hung. Below decks the first crew lunch was already being prepared in the ship's sparkling new stainless steel kitchens. From being an empty steel shell taking shape in the dry dock a year earlier the *Queen Elizabeth* was already home to her resident community of nearly a thousand people.

While the new *Queen Elizabeth*'s crew were moving aboard their new ship, Allison and Derek were moving out of their home in Winnetka and into a luxury apartment in a landmark Mies van der Rohe building on central Chicago's Lake Shore Drive. Gillian, who by then had obtained her Doctorate in English Literature and was teaching at the University of Manitoba in Winnipeg, flew to Chicago for a few days to help her parents move and settle into their new home. As they sorted through the house's contents Allison gave to Gill the huge boxed album containing all of her memories of that 1948 crossing on the old *Queen Elizabeth* that had brought the family to America more than 60 years earlier. It had always been one of Gill's favourite rainy-day pastimes as a child to sit at the dining room table and look through those pages, and she was thrilled to now have this treasure as a gift to take home.

With her parents comfortably ensconced in their new home, Gill kept the album with her as a carry-on item during the flight back to Winnipeg. It was a point of conversation with the lady in the seat beside her, who told Gill that there was a new *Queen Elizabeth* being built in Italy and she had a friend in Toronto who was writing a book about it. There were still some blank pages at the end of that album and she thought it would be a nice idea to fill them, so the next morning Gill called her travel agent and booked a short summer cruise for the following year from New York on the new *Queen Elizabeth* for herself and Allison – Derek was never too keen on being at sea and would be quite happy to stay at home, look after the two cats and maybe do a bit of watercolour painting in his new surroundings.

Top: The completed Verandah Restaurant has a richer and warmer palette than shown in the architect's digital rendering shown on page 59. (Brian David Smith)

Above: Cunard Executive Chef Jean-Marie Zimmermann chats informally with guests in the Verandah Restaurant for which he has himself created the specialised cuisine. (Cunard)

CHAPTER 5

THE QUEEN ELIZABETH MAKES HER DEBUT

CUNARD

QUEEN ELIZABETH

The *Queen Elizabeth* was officially handed over to Cunard in a short open-air ceremony on the ship's top deck on Thursday 30th September 2010 with the signing of legal documents by Fincantieri's Monfalcone Shipyard Director Cesare De Marco and Carnival UK CEO David Dingle, witnessed by Cunard's Peter Shanks and the ship's Captain Christopher Wells. As the *Queen Elizabeth* so changed hands, nationality and registry, the Italian Flag was lowered from atop the main mast and the Red Ensign, the flag of the British Merchant Navy run up in its place by Third Officer Matthew Wilson. The Cunard House Flag and an Italian Flag, signifying that the ship was in an Italian port, were flown beneath to either side of the mast crosstree. Following the ceremony the *Queen Elizabeth* was prepared for her departure for Southampton, at 15.30 hours under a pale Mediterranean afternoon sun. As the *Queen Elizabeth* manoeuvred away from the shipyard pier, crew and guests aboard lined the deck rails to cheer the Fincantieri workers and staff who had gathered to wish the new Cunarder bon voyage.

During the passage to Southampton final preparations were made on board for her official naming by HM The Queen on Monday 11th October and for her entry into revenue-earning commercial service the following day. Retail merchandise was priced and put on display in Fortnum's, Ocean Books and the Royal Arcade's other fine shops, while the hair styling and beauty salons and the spa operations were made ready to receive their first patrons. Brand new medical equipment was unpacked, set up and tested, while the dispensary shelves were stocked in the ship's medical centre, and library books were catalogued and shelved. Paintings and other art pieces placed in front of their designated places were hung and secured, while bathroom linens, toiletries and bathrobes were distributed to 1,046 passenger cabins and suites. The ship arrived in Southampton the following Friday morning ready

to go into service almost immediately, but first she was to receive a thousand invited overnight dinner guests for the Royal naming ceremony and then start her first commercial voyage the next day.

As befits Great Britain's rich maritime history and traditions, the Royal Family has long been actively interested in maritime and naval matters. At the age of 11 years HRH Princess Elizabeth accompanied her father, HM George VI on the old Royal Yacht *Victoria and Albert* when he reviewed The Fleet at Spithead as King for the first time in 1937. The following year she attended the first *Queen Elizabeth*'s launching at Clydebank. As the throne passed to Elizabeth after George VI's death on 6th February 1952, one of the many responsibilities to be taken up by the new Monarch was the *Victoria and Albert*'s replacement. Her late father had already approved the Admiralty's overall plan for a modern Royal Yacht, designed in a contemporary passenger ship style.

Like newlyweds planning a country home for their young family, The Queen and Duke of Edinburgh took a detailed interest in the design and building of the Royal Yacht *Britannia*, completed by John Brown & Co, Clydebank in 1954. As a naval officer himself, The Duke of Edinburgh offered many suggestions on the ship's technical and operational design based on practical experience and his knowledge of both naval and merchant ship design. Together the young Royal couple created what was to be an ocean-going state residence, with all the facilities of Buckingham Palace or Sandringham House from the private Royal apartments to the state reception rooms, guest accommodations and support services for running the monarchy from anywhere they might be in the world right down to the knighting stool used for investitures during their world travels.[18]

In addition to the Royal Yacht *Britannia*, Cunard's QE2 and new *Queen Elizabeth*, other major British passenger liners launched by The Queen include the Shaw Savill & Albion

85

*Top: An Italian tug salutes the **Queen Elizabeth** as she makes her way into the open waters of the Adriatic for her delivery voyage. (Brian David Smith)*

*Above: As an early-morning fog lifts on 8th October 2010, Cunard's new **Queen Elizabeth** is given a traditional fireboat welcome in brilliant sunshine as she makes her way up Southampton Water for the first time. (Andrew Cooke)*

Line's aft-engined Southern Cross at Harland & Wolff's Queen's Island yard in 1954 and Union Castle Line's last express liner for the Cape Town service, Windsor Castle at Cammell Laird in Birkenhead in 1959. Of P&O Orient Line's *Oriana* and *Canberra*, the two largest British-built liners built during the fifties and sixties, *Oriana* was launched by Princess Alexandra at Vickers Armstrong's Barrow yard in 1959, while the *Canberra*, named for Australia's capital city was launched by Dame Pattie Menzies, the nation's First Lady at the time. The Queen had originally been asked to perform the honour but had ultimately declined as she would be in the advanced stages of her pregnancy with Prince Andrew at the time.[19] P&O's second *Oriana*, built at Meyer Werft in Papenburg, Germany was officially named by The Queen in 1995 on the ship's arrival at Southampton following her delivery voyage from the yard. Throughout her reign The Queen has also launched numerous other naval and commercial vessels of all types.

The Royal Family has also maintained a relationship with the *QE2* and her company, visiting the ship a number of times during the ship's distinguished career of nearly 40 years, as The Queen Mother had done with the first *Queen Elizabeth*. The 1990 Royal Review of the Fleet paid a special tribute to Cunard for the 150-year anniversary of the Line's founding in 1840, with the *QE2*, *Vistafjord* and the new container cargo ship *Atlantic Conveyor* replacing her earlier namesake lost in the Falklands conflict included in the Review. Following the Review itself, The Queen and Prince Philip transferred by launch from the Royal Yacht *Britannia* to the *QE2* for the liner's return to Southampton. During the hour or so the Royal couple spent as highly honoured guests of Cunard they made a walkabout through the ship's public areas to meet delighted passengers and crew. This is the only occasion when a reigning British monarch has travelled aboard a commercial passenger liner with paying passengers also aboard.[20] The

Plumes of water from the tug Svitzer Sussex play into the air as the **Queen Elizabeth** *slows to make an unassisted 180-degree turn to enter her berth at Southampton's Ocean Dock. (Cunard)*

Duke of Edinburgh made a final farewell visit to the *QE2* on the day of her departure for Dubai and planned conversion there for use in a static role as a hotel and tourist attraction.

Right on cue the newest Cunard *Queen* broke out from a light early-morning fog into brilliant sunshine as she made her way up Southampton Water towards her new home port for the first time. Surrounded by tugs playing jets of sparkling water into the bright chill morning air from their powerful fire hoses and a veritable flotilla of excursion boats and pleasure craft of all sorts, the new Cunarder turned herself around a full 180 degrees in the Lower Swinging Ground of Southampton Docks under her own computerised controls to manoeuvre astern in alongside Berth 47 at the new Ocean Terminal.

During the weekend final preparations were made on board the *Queen Elizabeth*, both for the naming ceremony and its related festivities, and for the maiden voyage that would begin the following day. Meanwhile on the quayside a 'Grand Arena' was being assembled for the occasion, with a stage, bandstand, parade ground and grandstand seating for two thousand invited guests, along with all the broadcast sound and lighting facilities for worldwide network television coverage of the event, with large-screen monitors being set up at several locations throughout the town of Southampton for the public to watch the event.

On Monday 11th October the Royal naming ceremony's guests checked in at the Ocean Terminal, first for a special luncheon aboard the ship and then for the ceremony itself, which unlike the *QM2* and *Queen Victoria* events, would be held outdoors in daylight on what turned out to be a

*Left: The new **Queen Elizabeth** lies alongside the new Ocean Terminal, with the town centre of Southampton in the background and the temporary stage and grandstand seating for the naming ceremony being completed on the pier beside her starboard bow. (Cunard)*

89

Cunard President and Managing Director Peter Shanks applauds as HM Queen Elizabeth II officially names the new ship in a televised afternoon ceremony on Monday 11th October 2010. (Cunard)

gloriously warm and sunny autumn afternoon. Upon their early-afternoon arrival the Royal party first made a tour of the ship, starting with the bridge, where Captain Christopher Wells introduced HM to his officers. There, The Queen pressed a button to sound the ship's whistles – the shortness of the blast from these seemed to show that Her Majesty, and just about everyone else, were somewhat surprise by the sound's great strength. During the tour The Queen asked to see one of the ship's suites, something that organisers had omitted from the programme. Her wish was obliged with a courteous, 'Of course Ma'am,' and a deft unseen flurry of activity began behind the scenes away from the Royal gaze to grant her wish, before a walkthrough in the Royal Court Theatre to meet the rest of the ship's company. HM The Queen, accompanied by Captain Christopher Wells, Cunard and Carnival executives and other dignitaries, then left the ship and made their way along the Grand Arena's parade ground for the naming itself.

The two thousand invited guests filling the grandstand were already being serenaded by the Bournemouth Symphony Orchestra and Chorus, the Band and Pipes of the Coldstream Guards, The Band of the Scots Guards and Trumpeters of the Irish Guards. In a short traditional ceremony, similar to that she had attended when her mother did the same honours for the first *Queen Elizabeth*'s 1938 launching at Clydeside, HM Queen Elizabeth II spoke the time-honoured words, 'I name this ship *Queen Elizabeth*: May God bless her and all who sail in her.' A magnum of Rothschild was swung against the ship's bows where it 'obliterated' as Peter Shanks hoped and prayed it would. Streamers were released and fireworks soared into the sky – Cunard's newest *Queen* had been officially and royally christened.

The Queen spent only 60 minutes aboard the ship and at the ceremonies, during which her presence warmed the hearts of all with her captivating smile and gracious personality. For the entire ship's company and other invited guests aboard

*The **Queen Elizabeth** pictured at South Queensferry during her first Round Britain Cruise on 4th September 2011. (Colin Smith)*

Queen Elizabeth, as she did a walkthrough in the Royal Court Theatre and Queen's Room, it was a 'moment' in their lifetimes to be so close to this highly revered and greatly loved reigning monarch. Musicians from the Bournemouth Symphony Orchestra spoke with BBC News later in the day of the immense sense of privilege they felt performing for The Queen so close to her in the Grand Arena that afternoon, while other guests told of the remarkable experience of actually singing the national anthem, God Save the Queen 'in the presence.'

As the Royal motorcade left Southampton's Ocean Terminal after the naming, celebrations continued with a black-tie dinner in the ship's Britannia and Grill restaurants, followed by entertainment in the Royal Court Theatre, dancing in the Queen's Room and Yacht Club and an overnight stay aboard the ship for a thousand honoured guests.

Later on that day following the naming ceremony, the

Queen Elizabeth embarked her first paying passengers for her maiden voyage, a 13-night cruise to the Canary Islands, followed by two Mediterranean cruises, a short Christmas markets voyage to Northern Europe and a Christmas cruise to the Caribbean before starting out on her first circumnavigation of the world in early 2011. All of this has a significant link with Cunard's heritage and history as the Atlantic Islands itinerary in particular is a veritable repeat of the *QE2*'s maiden cruise in April 1969, before she made her first round trip crossing to New York. Without being earmarked for the *QM2*'s seasonal transatlantic line services, but rather the type of cruise service for which the *QE2* became so well known, these first Atlantic Island and world cruises are a favourable omen of the good fortune and hopes of a long and distinguished career that awaits the brand new *Queen Elizabeth.*

*Top: The Red Ensign flies beside the Italian flag atop the **Queen Elizabeth**'s mast as she is handed over from her Italian builders to her new British owners. (Brian David Smith)*

*Above: Seen here against the distant Italian countryside, the bridge's starboard-side control console aboard the **Queen Elizabeth** awaits the skilled hands of ship's officers that imminently will take her to sea and into commercial service. (Brian David Smith)*

REFERENCES

1   Bonsor, North Atlantic Seaway, p. 32

2   Maxtone-Graham, The Only Way to Cross, p. 394

3   Potter and Frost, The Elizabeth, p. 103

4   Warwick, *QE2*, p. 46

5   Stevens, The Elizabeth: Passage of a Queen, p. 42

6   Maxtone-Graham, The Only Way to Cross, p. 5

7   Owen, The Grand Days of Travel, p. 25

8   K. T. Rawland, Steam at Sea, p. 200

9   Murray Hughes, Die Hochgeschwindigkeits Story, p. 19

10   Harry Holland, Travellers' Architecture, p. 17

11   Potter and Frost, *QE2*: The authorized story, p. 15

12   Potter and Frost, The Elizabeth, p. 22

13   Bruce Peter, Philip Dawson, Ian Johnston, *QE2*: Britain's greatest liner, p. 49

14   BBC Scotland television documentary *QE2*: The last great liner

15   The Telegraph (online), 'Rising Star: Isobel Peachey, artist' 12th March 2010

16   Davis Piper, The Companion Guide to London, p. 36

17   Nils Schwerdtner, Die Neuen Queens der Cunard Line, p. 155-6

18   Richard Johnstone-Bryden, Britannia: The official history, p. 13

19   Philip Dawson, Canberra: In the wake of a legend, p. 45

20   Southern Daily Echo Newspapers, *QE2*: A celebration of forty years service, p. 93

QUEEN ELIZABETH - CUNARD LINE, SOUTHAMPTON

Builders: Fincantieri, Monfalcone Yard, Italy

Keel laid: 6th July 2009

Floated out: 5th January 2010

Delivered: 30th September 2010

Fincantieri Yard number: 6187

IMO number: 9477438

Flag: United Kingdom

Port of registry: Southampton

Classification: Lloyd's Register +100A1

Overall dimensions

Length overall: 294.0 m

Waterline length: 265.36 m

Beam: 32.36 m

Draft: 7.9 m

Air draft (Height above waterline): 55.07 m

Depth to bulkhead deck (A Deck): 10.80 m

Depth to Promenade Deck (3 Deck): 19.81 m

Measure and capacities

Gross tonnage (GT): 90,000

Passengers, lower berths: 2,092

Passenger accommodations: 1,046 cabins and suites, 86% with outside exposure, 71% with private verandas

Officers and crew: 1005

Fuel capacity: 3,456 m2

Fresh water capacity: 3,150 m2

Machinery and performance

Power: 6 diesel generator sets in total generating 63,380 kW of electrical power.

Propulsion: 2 azimuthing propeller pods yielding a total motive power of 35,200 kW

Trial speed: 24.3 knots

Service speed: 21.7 knots

Fuel consumption: 240 tonnes heavy fuel oil per 24 hours

Manoeuvring: 2 transverse bow thrusters used in conjunction with the pods for docking

Stabilisation: 2 retractable anti-rolling fins

*A foretelling of the **Queen Elizabeth**'s maiden arrival in Sydney, Australia against a backdrop of the Opera House and the Sydney Harbour Bridge as depicted in this Robert Lloyd painting. (Courtesy of Cunard)*

ACKNOWLEDGEMENTS

The planning, design, construction and commissioning of a great deep sea passenger ship such as the *Queen Elizabeth* is the result of teamwork among various professions, disciplines, trades and skills, bringing together the creativity and hard work of literally thousands of people in Great Britain, Italy, the United States, Sweden and elsewhere. And so too the creation even of a modest volume such as this about the ship is likewise the veritable harvest of teamwork and collaboration, albeit on a considerably smaller scale.

We are especially grateful to Brian David Smith for all of his outstanding photography of the *Queen Elizabeth*'s building at Monfalcone right from the time the first steel was cut through to the ship's completion and handover to Cunard and departure on her delivery voyage to keep her naming engagement with Her Majesty The Queen in Southampton. Brian has worked tirelessly to capture every aspect of the Elizabeth's gestation and delivery, making numerous trips to the Fincantieri Monfalcone Yard, gaining access to various parts of the yard, including the tops even of its cranes and into the unfinished interiors of the ship as she has taken shape there. We are privileged as well to include several outstanding Robert Lloyd paintings of both the first and new *Queen Elizabeth's* including a remarkable fore-showing of the new ship's maiden arrival in Sydney, Australia as part of her first world cruise, and once again we sincerely appreciate both John Hendy's and Bruce Peter's contribution of archival photographs.

Our sincere thanks also go to the people of Fincantieri's Monfalcone Yard for the hospitality they have extended to Brian and for their help with additional images and information as required. From the shipowners' side we wish to thank in particular Michael Gallagher, Public Relations Executive, for his support and his efforts in securing additional information and access to company resources during times of great demand on his resources and Stephen Payne Vice President and Chief Naval Architect, Carnival Shipbuilding, as ever, for his kind assistance with technical information. Thanks also to Caroline Hallworth for her careful and thorough proofing and editing of the text, to Clare Price at Lily Publications for her resourcefulness and to Rebecca Money at Ocean Books for her support. I shall also be eternally grateful to my good friend and neighbour Gillian Teiman for her thoughtful suggestions. Finally our thanks to John Lewis and his team of Gomer Press for printing the book in a 48 hour period to meet the deadline for the maiden voyage.

Once again, it has been a great pleasure to work with Miles and Linda Cowsill and the whole team in the Isle of Man on this my second work with Lily Publications.